50

The Berkshire Studies in European History

GENERAL EDITORS

RICHARD A. NEWHALL
LAURENCE B. PACKARD
SIDNEY R. PACKARD

Berkshire Studies in European History

Under the Editorship of
Richard A. Newhall, Laurence B. Packard and Sidney R. Packard

IMPERIALISM AND NATIONALISM IN THE FAR EAST

BY

DAVID EDWARD OWEN

ASSOCIATE PROFESSOR OF HISTORY
YALE UNIVERSITY

NEW YORK
HENRY HOLT AND COMPANY

PREFACE

The college teacher of general European history is always confronted with the task of finding adequate reading for his classes which is neither too specialized and technical nor too elementary. For many topics, including several of the greatest importance, no such material is at the moment available. Moreover, in too many instances, good reading which undeniably does exist is in the form of a chapter in a larger work and is therefore too expensive for adoption as required reading under normal conditions.

The Berkshire Studies in European History have been planned to meet this situation. The topics selected for treatment are those on which there is no easily accessible reading of appropriate length adequate for the needs of a course in general European history. The authors, all experienced teachers, are in nearly every instance actively engaged in the class room and intimately acquainted with its problems. They will avoid a merely elementary presentation of facts, giving instead an interpretive discussion suited to the more mature point of view of college students.

No pretense is made, of course, that these *Studies* are contributions to historical literature in the scholarly sense. Each author, nevertheless, is sufficiently a specialist in the period of which he writes to be familiar with the sources and to have used the latest scholarly contributions to his subject. In order that those who desire to read further on any topic may have some guidance short bibliographies of works in western European languages are given, with particular attention to books of recent date.

Each *Study* is designed as a week's reading. The division into three approximately equal chapters, many of them self-contained and each suitable for one day's assignment, should make the series as a whole easily adaptable to the present needs of college classes. The editors have attempted at every point to maintain and emphasize this fundamental flexibility.

Maps and diagrams will occasionally be furnished with the text when specially needed but a good historical atlas, such as that of Shepherd, is presupposed throughout.

R. A. N.
L. B. P.
S. R. P.

CONTENTS

IMPERIALISM AND NATIONAL-
ISM IN THE FAR EAST

CHAPTER I

THE EXCLUSIVE EAST AND THE EXPANDING WEST

A CHINESE chronicler of the sixteenth century records the arrival of a party of strange beings who "came to Macao in two or three large ships. Their clothes and their hair were red; their bodies were tall; they had blue eyes sunk deep in their heads. Their feet were one cubit and two-tenths long; and they frightened the people by their strange appearance." This image of our European ancestors, reflected in an Oriental mirror, is quite as significant a revelation of the Chinese themselves as of the Westerners who so offended their sense of beauty. Nor is it a matter for surprise that foreigners should be regarded as curious creatures by the men of China, for throughout the 2,500 years of their recorded history, contacts with the West have been relatively infrequent and ephemeral. Indeed, of the three great seats of early civilization, the Mediterranean area, India, and China, the last was by all odds the least subject to foreign influence. European civilization is plainly a composite of almost innumerable elements. Between Europe and India intercourse has continued with but few interruptions. But for China and Japan, isolation has produced a culture peculiarly their own.

The seclusion of the Far East has been determined

in a large measure by its geography. Until the sea came to be used extensively, China was all but inaccessible to Europeans. On most of its land frontier, the Empire was enclosed by a ring of lofty plateaus and mountains, through which passage was exceedingly difficult. To be sure, Chinese silks were highly prized by Greeks and Romans. Critics have discovered traces of Græco-Indian influence in Chinese art, while ancient geographers make mention of the great empire of the Far East, but in terms that are far from precise. Indeed, the following statement represents the total knowledge of the West in regard to the East about the year 500:

"The region of the Seres [China] is a vast and populous country, touching on the east the ocean and the limits of the habitable world; and extending west nearly to . . . the confines of Bactria. The people are civilized men, of mild, just, and frugal temper; eschewing collisions with their neighbors, and even shy of close intercourse, but not averse to dispose of their own products, of which raw silk is the staple, but which include also silk stuffs, furs, and iron of remarkable quality." [1]

Much of this early trade, however, was carried on indirectly, with the Arabs or other Near Eastern peoples acting as intermediaries. The Arabs, indeed, as early as the seventh century, established a colony at Canton. In the seventh century also, Nestorian Christianity [2] from Syria was introduced into northwestern China and for a time at least appears to have

[1] This quotation (Sir Henry Yule in the *Encyclopedia Britannica*) is a composite statement of ancient references to China.
[2] The Nestorian Christians were followers of the heretical patriarch of Constantinople, who was excluded from the episcopate and anathematized by the Council of Ephesus (431).

enjoyed some degree of prosperity. Almost all traces of this sect have now disappeared save for a remarkable tablet, which discloses the story of this earliest Christian mission. During the period of the Mongol dynasty (1280-1368 A.D.) the caravan route across Central Asia, the historic *Seidenstrasse* (silk route), was traversed by numbers of European traders, whose rich cargoes of silk went to supply the growing demand of an awakened Europe for luxuries. It was also during the rule of the Mongols that the early Franciscans and the picturesque Venetian globe-trotter, Marco Polo, enjoyed the hospitality of the Great Khan. After the collapse of the Mongol state, the land route was again closed, and not until early modern times did foreign influences again play upon the civilization of China.[3] The effect of these sporadic contacts was almost negligible, and the magnificent culture developed in China represents, in a unique sense, the genius of the Chinese people.

Isolation and the resulting ignorance of other civilizations bred in the Chinese mind a contempt for them. Foreigners were habitually referred to as "barbarians." Embassies from foreign courts were regarded as tribute-bearing inferiors, for China's diplomatic relations had been limited to receiving tribute from the semi-civilized border peoples. Diplomatic missions from Western nations were sent from the coast to Peking over the route reserved for tribute embassies. When presentation was made at the throne, there was

[3] The Mongols had managed to keep open the overland routes, but as their power waned the Ottoman Turks completely severed the land connection between Europe and the Far East.

inevitable trouble over the *kotow*, an obeisance which indicated absolute submission.[4]   Europeans usually refused to take part in a ceremony which they considered an affront, while the Chinese insisted that the Occidental, like the Burman or the Tartar, was an unspeakable barbarian come to seek the favor of the Son of Heaven. Just as every country which is deprived of contacts with other peoples comes to look upon itself as of transcendent importance in the scheme of the universe and regards the ways of foreigners as vulgar and uncouth, so the Chinese conceived countries other than their own as sunk in outer darkness.   Their most common term for China is *Chung Kuo*, literally "Middle Kingdom," the center of the world.   Probably there is no more candid statement of this traditional attitude than that made by the great Manchu emperor, Ch'ien Lung, when late in the eighteenth century, an embassy from the Court of St. James came to request certain trade concessions.   He patronizes George III in a fashion which to Western eyes seems both presumptuous and absurd.

"If you assert that your reverence for our Celestial dynasty fills you with a desire to acquire our civilization—our ceremonies and laws differ so completely from your own that, even if your envoy were able to acquire the rudiments of our civilization, you could not possibly transport our manners and customs to your alien soil. . . . We possess all things.   I set no value on objects strange or ingenious, and have expounded my wishes in detail and have commanded your tribute envoys to leave in peace on their homeward journey.   It behooves you, O King, to respect my sen-

[4] One who performed the *kotow* knelt three times, each time knocking his head thrice against the floor.

timents and to display even greater loyalty in the future. . . ."

Then, apparently regretting his asperity, in a second message Ch'ien Lung naïvely seeks to make amends:

"I do not forget the lonely remoteness of your island, cut off from the world by intervening wastes of sea, nor do I overlook your excusable ignorance of the usages of our Celestial Empire. I have consequently commanded my ministers to enlighten your ambassador on the subject. . . ." [5]

THE OLD CHINA

Chinese history is commonly regarded as having begun in a semi-mythical period about 2900 B.C. This was the age of the legendary Five Rulers, whose virtues were lavishly extolled by Confucius and the other philosophers. During its earliest days the empire was confined to a small area in the basin of the Yellow River, the cradle of Chinese civilization. By about 1100 B.C. the historian finds his footing somewhat less precarious, and he discovers a China in the hands of a dynasty that was to rule, at least nominally, for nine centuries. This régime may be compared roughly to that of feudalism in Europe. Feudal princes, as always, found much to disagree about, and civil wars were incessant. But, despite political confusion, it was the great formative age in a cultural sense. The most distinguished of the philosophers flourished, and Chinese civilization became crystallized. About 200 B.C. the country was consolidated under a single gov-

[5] Quoted in Hodgkin, *China in the Family of Nations,* pp. 52-53.

ernment, and the political history of the unified China began.

Twice the entire Middle Kingdom has been ruled by alien dynasties, but in each case the conquest was purely military. The invaders, victorious by force of arms, were in turn conquered by the superior culture of the Chinese. During the thirteenth century of our era China became a part of the great Mongol Empire, which stretched from the Black Sea on the west to the Yellow Sea on the east. Kublai Khan, the founder of the Mongol dynasty in China, proved to be one of the ablest of monarchs and extraordinarily receptive to European influences.

Again in the seventeenth century the empire fell prey to foreign rule. The Manchus had formed one of a group of warlike tribes whose relentless pressure upon the northern border was a perennial problem for Chinese rulers and against whom the Great Wall was constructed. With scarcely more than a rudimentary culture of their own, they displayed great acumen in organizing the government, appropriating Chinese customs, and enlisting Chinese ability in the administration. But ultimate control was retained in Manchu hands. This alien dynasty produced some leaders of great ability, but by the nineteenth century it had so deteriorated that its tenure, even before the coming of the West in force, was uncertain.

THE GOVERNMENT OF THE OLD CHINA

The historic political system of China offers a marked contrast to Western forms. It represents a curious blending of the divine-right ideal with the modern theory of the utilitarian state of Montesquieu and Bentham.[6] At the head of the government stood the emperor, in theory, absolute and paternal. But in contrast to the subjects of a Louis XIV who might only bow before the inscrutable edicts of Providence, when a ruler grew intolerable the Chinese could always organize a rebellion which, if successful, was interpreted as carrying out the decree of heaven. The usurper would therefore rule with the same divine sanction as his predecessor. This engaging bit of casuistry reveals the Chinese mind as essentially practical.

The real strength of the government, however, centered not in the patriarchal emperor but in a highly organized bureaucracy selected by competitive examination and composed of men of scholarly attainments, if not necessarily of administrative ability. Choice was based upon literary style and familiarity with the Chinese classics—the writings of Confucius and the other philosophers—and competition was open even to members of the humblest families. To be sure, such examinations inevitably placed a premium upon slavish memorizing and a stilted literary style, but at least they assured the Chinese people of a government whose agents were chosen by merit rather than by birth. The men selected in this fashion were assigned to the provinces in various capacities, and upon them de-

[6] The divine-right state is one which exists by supernatural sanction. In theory, it is the form of government ordained by God, against which mere men have no right to protest. On the other hand, the criterion by which the utilitarian state is judged is the welfare of its subjects. The utilitarian insists not that government conform to a divinely prescribed plan but that it be adapted to the needs of the people and conducive to human happiness.

volved most of the responsibility for the administration, since the central government confined itself largely to reviewing and criticizing their acts.

The loyalties connected with the Chinese political system were strikingly different from the patriotism of the West. National feeling was all but unknown until it was created by contact with Europeans. There were particularist loyalties, to the province, to the village, and to the family. Notwithstanding such favoring circumstances as homogeneity of race and written language, genuine unity was prevented by the almost insuperable obstacles of size, lack of rapid communication, and a multiplicity of spoken dialects. In administration the province was the most important unit, and provincial affairs were often conducted with considerable independence of the capital. Localism was further encouraged by the strength of family and village government, for much more effective than either emperor or bureaucracy was the democratic autonomy of the village and the patriarchal family. The key to Chinese society is to be found, therefore, in the family unit, which included not only father, mother, and children, but more distant relatives as well. Several generations might live together in one large house, where tablets in the home or in the ancestral hall recalled to the living the veneration due the dead members of the family group. The central position of the family was recognized also in the Chinese legal system. If one member of the family were convicted of a crime, the punishment, nicely graduated according to the degree of relationship, might be inflicted upon his relatives for having neglected the moral education of

the culprit. This conception of family solidarity per-
vades the entire Chinese social and political system.[7]

INDUSTRY AND AGRICULTURE

The utilitarian character of the Chinese mind is
further emphasized by the highly developed economic
life of the empire. Agriculture is the occupation of the
majority of the population, and it has been made an
art by the patient Chinese farmer, who is usually a
peasant proprietor. His implements may be exceedingly crude, but he is nevertheless a painstaking,
efficient cultivator. The very fact that the same ground
has been made to bear abundantly for thirty and perhaps forty centuries testifies to the way in which
fertility has been preserved. Canal mud and legumes
are employed extensively. Indeed, it is a common
practise to grow clover in rice fields immediately after
the crop has been harvested. The clover is then mixed
with canal mud and spread over the land in preparation
for a new rice planting. The Chinese have chosen
their crops with care. Wherever the rainfall or opportunities for irrigation make it possible, rice is grown.
In dry portions of the country other grains are staple,
especially millet, which is highly resistant to drought.
In short, the Chinese peasant, schooled in the experience of generations, is an intensive and intelligent
farmer.

The predominance of agriculture, however, did not
prevent the growth of an industrial and commercial life

[7] For a brief description of the family system, see Latourette,
The Development of China, pp. 133-35, on which the above is
based.

quite similar to that of Europe during the Middle Ages. Industries were small and were often carried on in shops, the fronts of which were used as salesrooms. Relations between master and apprentices were intimate and frequently cordial. As in medieval Europe certain streets in the Chinese city were occupied by craftsmen representing a particular trade, and in the empire as a whole various regions tended to specialize in the manufacture of certain products.

Tradesmen and craftsmen were organized into gilds, self-governing bodies for the encouragement and protection of economic activities. The provincial gilds were composed of tradesmen and workers from one province who were sojourning in another. The trade gilds, on the other hand, were analogous to the European craft gilds. They regulated production, prices, and conditions of apprenticeship, and their jurisdiction over individual members was considerable. In fact, civil cases at law were usually settled by the gild rather than by the magistrates. For a land as large as China there was a surprising volume of intersectional trade. Navigable rivers and canals, of which there were many thousands of miles, formed the principal avenues of trade, but these were supplemented by roads, some of which were kept in excellent condition.

CHINESE PHILOSOPHY AND RELIGION

The civilization of China was shaped, in large measure, by the teachings of the philosophers, particularly those of Confucius (about 500 B.C.) and his followers. Confucian thought dictated not only the ethics of the family system, but became the final arbiter in all social, political, and economic relations as well. In a sense, it is a misnomer to call Confucius a philosopher. He was not preoccupied with the philosophical abstractions which have interested thinkers in the West. Rather was he an ethical teacher, enunciating the principles of private and public morality. His emphasis was on the duty of children to parents, of wives to husbands, and of citizens to the state. With its great precept, "What you do not like yourself, do not do to others," Confucian philosophy promulgated an exceedingly high ethical code. Like Jesus and Gautama Buddha, Confucius taught by the Socratic method, answering questions as they were put to him and discussing them with his followers. His disciples took down his sayings and wrote commentaries upon them. This body of writings literally set the mold in which Chinese civilization was to be cast during subsequent centuries.

A scarcely distinguishable line separates Chinese philosophy from Chinese religion. Confucianism is not, strictly speaking, a religion, although it contains religious elements. But the major emphasis of the Confucian school was upon duty to fellow man rather than to deity. It was essentially this-worldly. The mystical, supernatural element was supplied largely by Taoism and Buddhism. The former was developed from the philosophy contained in a book, the *Tao Tê Ching*, roughly contemporary with Confucius. Originally Taoism represented the contemplative, otherworldly outlook on life, but to-day its doctrines have become so confused with superstition and demonology that they exert little influence upon the educated.

Buddhism, of course, was an importation from India, but it thrived on the soil of China, to which it was first transplanted about 250 B.C. Gautama Buddha (about 500 B.C.), its founder, taught that in the extermination of desire and striving lay the road to spiritual peace. But what was originally an exalted ethical code tended to become, in China, a debased mysticism. The average Chinese, however, gives his allegiance to no one of the sects, but shrewdly seeks the benefit of all. He "is at once an animist, a Confucianist, a Buddhist, and a Taoist without any sense of inconsistency. His ethics are Confucian or Buddhist; he calls in Buddhist or Taoist priests at critical times of illness or burial; and he honors the names of his ancestors, propitiates evil spirits, and seeks blessings from beneficent ones" (Latourette). Animism or belief in spirits seems to have been for the mass of the people the effective religion.

LITERATURE AND ART

Even apart from the writings of the great sages, the literature of China is of great volume. The Chinese regard the written character with almost superstitious reverence. "Scraps of paper with characters inscribed on them must be preserved with care or destroyed with decorum" (Hodgkin). Only recently has the beauty of Chinese poetry been recognized in the West, so difficult is the work of translation. The following fragment is the work of Li Tai-po (eighth century A.D.), one of a group of congenial souls who lived on the side of the Chu Lai mountain and who called themselves, quite properly, "The Eight Immortals of the Wine-

Cup." The lyrics of Li are distinguished by a delicate buoyancy and a sensitiveness to beauty in the mountain, the forest, and the "jade-green waterfall."

> "To-night I stay at the Summit Temple.
> Here I could pluck the stars with my hand.
> I dare not speak aloud in the silence,
> For fear of disturbing the dwellers of heaven." [8]

Between 700 and 900 A.D., the golden age of Chinese poetry, some nine hundred volumes were produced. History also received its share of attention. Events, chiefly those dealing with official life, were recorded in great detail by chroniclers, a few of whom used critical methods. In order to avoid the writing of eulogistic history, the record of each dynasty was set down only after it had been overthrown.

The art of China, unlike its poetry, has long been admired in the West. Delicacy of coloring and depth of feeling are present in the best of the landscape painting. The Gothic architect dedicated his handiwork to the Church, the Renaissance painter found his great inspiration in human beings, but to the Chinese artist both God and man were subordinated to the great harmonies of nature, which the painter suggests by a few strokes of the brush rather than by reproducing in servile fashion the details of the actual scene. In their porcelains and potteries, even more than in their painting, the Chinese, "the greatest race of potters the world has ever seen," have taken a commanding position, and they have contributed the name "china," which the Occident applies to the best of its

[8] From *The Poems of Li Po,* translated by S. Obata. E. P. Dutton & Company.

tableware. They first developed the technique for making delicate, translucent porcelains, which they covered with rich glazes of olive green or soft blue or the glorious red known as *sang de boeuf*. Their porcelain vessels were often decorated with painted designs in luminous cobalt blue or dazzling copper red, fired on over the glaze. In jade and bronze, in lacquer and enamel, the work of the Chinese suggests the happy union of sound, painstaking craftsmanship with an inspired artistic instinct.

Architecture has assumed a much less important place in the artistic expression of the Chinese than have painting and ceramics, and the greatest of their structures impress one as the work of the painter rather than the architect. But such a building as the imperial palace at Peking is properly regarded as a masterpiece of detail. The countryside is dotted with pagodas, whose shimmering roofs, with their self-assertive corners and graceful curves, reveal a people to whom beauty is no alien.

THE OLD JAPAN

The civilization of China deserves a more appreciative understanding in the West not only for its inherent worth but also because it furnished the framework for the culture developed in the islands to the east. The naïve legends of the Japanese, like most racial mythologies, ascribe their origin to the gods themselves. Ethnologists, however, are unable to state with certainty the source of the islanders. A series of migrations from the mainland, some possibly from the

East Indies, seems to have supplied most of the racial stock. From the beginning Japan was a military state, since the island had to be conquered from the aborigines, and, once subjugated, had to be defended against attempts to reclaim it. Almost from the first the institution of the emperor was present, not, to be sure, in its later form, but merely as a shadowy suzerainty over various subordinate chieftains and as co-ordinator of the military forces. The continuity of the imperial institution is of the utmost importance, for it represents the great link between the ancient and the modern Japan and makes the new appear a flowering of the old.

During her early history Japan was decisivly affected by two foreign influences. About 400 A.D. the culture of China and the religion of Buddha crossed the Yellow Sea hand in hand, and the former at least was eagerly received by the islanders, whose civilization was still in a rudimentary stage. The Japanese here displayed the same capacity for assimilating a foreign culture that was later to ease their entrance into the family of modern nations. But theirs was not slavish imitation. It is true that, for a time, the worship of things Chinese threatened to become a cult. The Japanese bowed down before the achievements of their neighbors much as the courts of Frederick the Great and Maria Theresa did fulsome homage to French fashions and manners. In the end, however, the islanders made that which they had borrowed their own. The written language was appropriated and adapted to meet Japanese needs. The treasures of Chinese literature were freely drawn upon and were the inspiration for a Japanese national literature. Confucian and Buddhist ethics were transformed into the chivalric code of the ruling class.

Buddhism, on the other hand, at first found itself on inhospitable soil; through the support of a noble family, however, it finally came to prevail. Yet even in its days of greatest popularity, Buddhism never completely superseded the older religion, Shinto or emperor-worship, which was later restored to a position of supremacy. But, it may be repeated, in contrast to the Westerner to whom religions are mutually exclusive, neither the average Japanese nor Chinese pins his hopes of salvation upon any one religion, but practises what seems to us a curious eclecticism.

THE GOVERNMENT OF THE OLD JAPAN

A glance at the political system of Japan before her westernization reveals a condition singularly like that which preceded modern nationalism in Europe. There was, as in China, an emperor who was theoretically absolute. During the eighth and ninth century of our era his power was growing weaker and weaker, while noble families dominated the scene. When the control of these nobles declined, the large landholders of the country arrogated an increasing degree of authority to themselves. Thus for the seven hundred years preceding its westernization, Japan was a feudal state. The emperor was a mere figure-head, to be venerated rather than obeyed, and power was concentrated in the hands of a military caste, always an important factor in a feudal state. The leader of this military class was called the shogun,[9] who was in fact ruler of the country and virtually independent of the emperor. The land was held by great *daimyo*, whose estates, frequently immune from the jurisdiction of the central government, were enfeoffed to vassals in return for military service. The *samurai* corresponded to the knight of European feudalism. He was usually attached to a chieftain and was ready to bear arms at the call of his lord.

THE IDEALS OF THE MILITARY CLASS

If the ethical standards of China were the work of the Confucian philosophers, it is scarcely less true to say that those of Japan were derived from the ideals of the military class. The code of the *samurai*, called *bushido*, is somewhat reminiscent of European chivalry. Though its canons were never reduced to writing and the *samurai* was judged only at the bar of his own conscience, the code represented a generally accepted basis for conduct. The Japanese knight was schooled in the Spartan virtue of stoical self-control, even under the most trying conditions. He must first master himself before he might engage his other foes in combat. In the words of a knight of the eleventh century,

> "Subdue first of all thy own self,
>   Next thy friends and last thy foes;
>   Three victories are these of him
>   That would a conqueror's name attain." [10]

[9] The shogunate originated late in the twelfth century. This institution, it will be seen, has certain points in common with that of the Merovingian *major domus*.

[10] Quoted in Nitobé, *The Japanese Nation*, p. 156.

Above all *bushido* inculcated what has been called the "religion of loyalty." This virtue took precedence over all others and over all natural ties. To his *daimyo* the *samurai* pledged all that he possessed, even life itself, and he could conceive of no destiny more exalted than that of dying for his feudal lord. The wearer of two swords—this privilege was reserved for *samurai* alone—must express his loyalty to lord and parents by his eagerness to avenge any wrong done to them. His sword must be unsheathed to defend virtue and to succor weakness. If under the cloud of disgrace, his only honorable course was self-destruction by disembowelment, which he effected with an elaborate ceremonial.[11] Although *bushido* applied specifically only to the nobility, its ideals tended to permeate all of Japanese society, however imperfectly they may have been observed even by the *samurai* themselves.

These virtues, which centered in the feudal bond, took the place of patriotic sentiment. Feudalism in Japan, as in Europe, "concealed in its bosom the weapons with which it would itself one day be smitten." It formally acknowledged the sovereignty of the emperor, even though in practise it might be supremely contemptuous of him. When conditions were ripe for a reassertion of imperial authority the feudal structure collapsed. Therefore, in the nominal supremacy of the emperor, the continuity with the past which he represented, and in the loyalty to the feudal chieftain, we find qualities readily transmuted into national patriotism. These, together with the innate adaptability

---

[11] *Hara kiri* or *seppuku,* as it is more often called by the Japanese themselves.

of the Japanese people, were to make Japan's entrance into the modern world a less painful experience than that of her unwieldy continental neighbor.

THE FAR EASTERN TRADE DURING EARLY MODERN TIMES

The establishment of direct commercial relations between the Orient and Western Europe represents a phase of the movement which we term the commercial revolution. The horizons of European life were expanding and were about to comprehend the entire world. The commercial spirit, on which had rested the prosperity of the Italian cities in the later Middle Ages, spread to the west, infecting the national states of the Atlantic seaboard. The welfare of these new monarchies, it was felt, depended upon a vigorous economic life, and in the bodies of capital which the commerce of previous centuries had accumulated were to be found the sinews for trade over larger areas. As a result of the breach between the Protestants and the Roman Church, the missionary zeal of the latter had been rekindled, so that with the Spanish and Portuguese *conquistadores* went Jesuit missionaries. Finally, and perhaps most important of all, a spirit of inquiry and curiosity seemed to revivify European life and to inspire people with a desire to know more of the world in which they lived. Vasco da Gama pointed to two of these factors when, as he set foot on shore at Calicut, he proclaimed, "We come for Christians and for spices."

When once the Portuguese navigators had discovered the direct sea route to India and were returning to Europe with the products of the East, it was inevitable

that attempts should be made to penetrate the fast-
nesses of the Middle Kingdom. During the sixteenth
century the government of China was by no means
conspicuously inhospitable toward foreigners. Jesuit
missionaries appeared at the imperial court, and, chiefly
because of their scientific learning and their readiness to
accommodate themselves to the customs of the country,
they stood high in the favor of the emperor. Indeed,
not until the barbarian traders had treated the Chinese
to some unedifying exhibitions of violence and avarice
were restrictive measures imposed upon their commerce.

In 1516 a Portuguese ship first arrived off the coasts
of China, followed by others in 1517 and 1518. These
early voyagers were quite unaware that they had at
last reached the Cathay which had lured European
explorers since the days of the epic Marco Polo. Their
reception was not harsh. In fact, one of their number
was welcomed by local officials at Canton and allowed
to proceed to Peking. Unfortunately the tactics of his
compatriots convinced the Chinese that their earlier
judgment had been all too charitable. The net result
was that the Portuguese finally confined their atten-
tions to Macao, an island near Canton, which they
rented for a long period of years and ultimately claimed
in full sovereignty. A half century after the Portuguese, arrived their kinsmen, the Spaniards, who came
from the West by way of the Philippines. Holding an
admirable trading base at Manila, they made little
effort to establish themselves on the mainland but
allowed Chinese merchants to come to the Philippines.
Early in the seventeenth century appeared repre-

sentatives of the Dutch East India Company. After
three attempts to appropriate territory on the mainland or on an adjacent island, they finally devoted
themselves to trading under regulations prescribed by
the Chinese government. In the wake of the Dutch
adventurers arrived the English. As early as 1596
Queen Elizabeth had despatched a letter to the emperor
of China, requesting that "these our subjects, when they
shall come for traffic's sake unto . . . your Empire,
they may have full liberty . . . of dealing in trade
and merchandise with your subjects. . . ." Unhappily
the bearers of this quaint document never reached the
coast of China, and it was not until 1637 that an English vessel entered a Chinese harbor. During the re-
mainder of the century the newcomers looked here and
there for a trading base. The Portuguese guarded their
monopoly at Macao with implacable jealousy, while
at other points where Chinese officials might be led to
tolerate them, conditions were generally unsatisfactory.
They managed to carry on some trade at Canton, in
spite of Portuguese intrigues against them, but not
until the middle of the eighteenth century was a permanent "factory" established. The English in China
represented the East India Company, to which had
been granted a monopoly of Far Eastern commerce. It
was not, therefore, until after the revolt of the American
colonies that their merchants entered the growing trade.
The first American vessel visited China in 1784.

CHINESE POLICY TOWARD FOREIGNERS

From the foregoing it may be gathered that official
China was not wholly cordial toward its insistent vis-

itors from the West. The latter had come uninvited, attracted by tales of the fabulous wealth of the Middle Kingdom. They demanded the silk, and later the tea, that China had to offer. The attitude of Peking varied from indifference to opposition, while that of local functionaries was determined largely by the size of the emoluments forthcoming from foreign merchants. The arrangements for trading operations were indeterminate, to say the least. With the exception of the Portuguese, the foreigners had wandered up and down the coast, sending futile embassies to Peking, most of which were never received by the Son of Heaven. There was no common ground for negotiation, since the Chinese government, unfamiliar with the ways of diplomatic intercourse, refused to enter into relations with the West.

In the middle of the eighteenth century, however, the emperor took a step which introduced a greater degree of order into the commercial contacts of the two civilizations. By an imperial edict he ordered all foreign commerce confined to the port of Canton. Henceforth the activities of the aggressive barbarian were to be restricted to a single city and the rest of the Middle Kingdom preserved from him.

SOME CHARACTERISTICS OF THE EARLY TRADE

At the point of the wedge that opened China stood the foremost commercial nation of the world, Great Britain. To be sure, traders from other countries were also included in the foreign community that grew up in Canton. In general, however, it was the British who carried on the major share of the trade, and it was the

British who attempted most vigorously to wrest commercial concessions from reluctant China. Other nations, such as the United States, were not loath to accept such advantages as the British were able to gain, but it was the latter who took the initiative.

During the eighteenth and most of the nineteenth centuries there were no attempts on the part of the British or of any other nation to capture the China market for themselves. One can scarcely regard this early attack upon the walls of China as a phase of imperialism. It was profitable trade, pure and simple, that was sought, and the merchants of all countries were loudly persistent in their demands for better commercial facilities. Mercantilism before 1800 had fallen into disrepute. Physiocrats and free traders piously hoped that economic internationalism would relieve Europe from the commercial conflicts that had disturbed the continent during the previous era. The policy of the British government, then, was dictated by the demand for commercial opportunity, not for territorial aggrandizement.

As for the Chinese, they had trade thrust upon them, and, officially at least, did nothing to encourage it. Commerce was not nearly so important to the East as to the West. The merchants of Europe and America desired to possess the tea and silk of China far more acutely than did the East require British textiles. Indeed, the trade at Canton was concerned chiefly with exports from China, and officials never wearied of reminding European merchants that the Chinese could do very well without manufactured goods. In only three years between 1792 and 1809 were British products sold at a profit in China. Nevertheless, trade with the West was enriching both Chinese merchants and Chinese officials, for Europe must bring specie to cover any unfavorable balance. In short, however contemptuous of Western intercourse officialdom might be for purposes of publicity, the true attitude, at least of the Canton administrators, is revealed by their solicitude for the trade whenever for one reason or another it was temporarily stopped. The actual policy of China, then, toward the commerce of the West was to accept it and rigidly to control it.

THE STATUS OF WESTERN MERCHANTS AT CANTON

The guardians of the barbarians during their stay in Canton were a group of Chinese merchants popularly known as the *co-hong*. They were responsible for the conduct of their wards, who must be instructed in the usages of the Middle Kingdom and whose turbulent ways must be carefully controlled. The *co-hong* acted as intermediary between the officials and the foreigners, for no officer of the Celestial Empire could negotiate with a mere trader. In return for accepting these obligations, the *co-hong* was granted a monopoly of all foreign commerce. Western merchants were subject to minute regulations. Their residence in Canton was tolerated only during the actual trading months, after which they must take up their abode in Portuguese Macao or leave Chinese waters altogether. Their personal freedom was curtailed in a variety of ways.

Naturally this state of affairs was not wholly satisfactory to the foreigners. Yet even with such a mass of annoying regulations, business was conducted in a fairly amicable fashion, save when officials interfered. The *hong* merchants gave many demonstrations of their probity, while the confidence which they possessed in the Canton representatives of the East India Company and other foreign firms of standing was significant. And, what was more, the trade was so profitable to the West that minor grievances could be borne fairly cheerfully. By the year 1832 there were some twenty firms, including ten British and seven American, doing business at Canton. The former, being debarred from trade between Great Britain and China by the Company's monopoly, devoted themselves to that between China and India. The supercargoes of the East India Company were responsible for the English community at Canton, and stood, in short, as quasi-consuls for the British government in China.[12]

THE PROBLEM OF DIPLOMATIC INTERCOURSE

To the Chinese the Company's monopoly probably represented as convenient an arrangement as could be devised. The supercargoes acted as sponsors for the entire foreign community, but they were not officials of the British government. Dealing with them, therefore, raised no unpleasant problems of diplomatic intercourse with the barbarian. But sentiment against the privileges of the Company both among the private mer-

[12] The term "supercargo" is usually applied, as the word would indicate, to the agent on board ship who is placed in charge of the cargo and its sale. Since in the early days the East India Company had no permanent factories in China, the supercargo came and departed with each vessel. The name, however, continued to be used for representatives of the Company in China even after they had become what, according to ordinary usage, we should call factors.

chants in China and in Great Britain became more and more threatening. At Canton the independent merchants chafed at the restrictions placed upon them and watched with envy the progress of the American trade, bound by no monopolistic fetters. In England the opposition was based both on grounds of theory and practise. The day of the great monopolistic companies had passed with the mercantilist dogma, and *laissez-faire* now occupied the minds of economists. Furthermore, there was the unpalatable fact that the East India Company had never made of China an important market for the woolens which the mills of Manchester were producing. The cries of British manufacturers became increasingly peremptory. Yet to their charges the Company might reply with perfect relevance that from English products shipped to Canton during twenty-three years, there had been realized only a loss of over eight million dollars.

Both attitudes are quite comprehensible. Great Britain herself was undergoing a revolution in her productive mechanism. The industrial revolution had enormously increased her capacity for production, and this surplus was seeking foreign markets. It was in reality the industrial revolution that was beating at the gates of China. Manufacturers in England, independent merchants in China, and *laissez-faire* theorists alike were products of the new age, and to these it was impossible for the Company to explain that the root of the difficulty was a highly developed "sales resistance" on the part of the Chinese.

The opponents of the Company unquestionably had the spirit of the age fighting with them, and they suc-

ceeded in carrying through Parliament a motion abol-
ishing the China monopoly of the East India Company
as of April 22, 1834. The British government itself
now assumed the responsibility of obtaining commercial favors for its citizens, sending to Canton officials
called superintendents of trade, who were vested with
ill-defined and amorphous powers. Obviously, the
new superintendent was an official vastly different
from a Company supercargo. Here was a diplomatic
representative demanding a reception as such. The
Chinese government had never received an ambassador
from the West on terms of equality, nor was there any
intention of negotiating with this latest arrival. The
appointment of superintendents of trade, therefore,
provided no solution for the fundamental question of
diplomatic intercourse.

THE PROBLEM OF JURISDICTION

Closely allied with the problem of equal diplomatic
intercourse was another question that had complicated
the relations of Chinese and foreigners almost from the
beginning, the problem of jurisdiction. Between two
states possessing similar legal systems and connected
by the regular channels of diplomatic relations, jurisdictional issues are relatively easy of settlement. The
law of the territory on which the offense is committed
is applied in each case. In China, however, the question was perennially troublesome. There were many
reasons why foreigners were reluctant to submit themselves to the Chinese legal code. They regarded the
law of China as but once removed from barbarism and
its administration as hopelessly inept and corrupt.

Essentially, the problem was one of conflict between two different sets of legal concepts. The West had adopted an individualistic law, under which the individual and only the individual was responsible for his acts. The Chinese, as we have seen, held to the doctrine of collective responsibility.[13] The corollary was that no crime might go unpunished. If the actual culprit could not be discovered, the vengeance of the state must be wreaked upon another. This principle was followed time after time by Chinese officials in punishing their countrymen for homicidal assaults upon foreigners, and they frequently sought to invoke it in dealing with the barbarians themselves. The conflict over jurisdiction is of the utmost significance, for it led to the establishment of the extra-territorial system, which the Chinese nationalists are attacking so vigorously.[14]

THE OPIUM QUESTION

The years immediately following the abolition of the Company's monopoly were marked by increasing friction between the two civilizations that confronted each other in the Far East. Foreign merchants, who, after the change in the status of the East India Company, were coming to China in augmented numbers,

[13] See above, p. 10.

[14] One of the most famous examples of legal conflict was the Terranova case. Terranova, a sailor on the American ship *Emily*, was held responsible by Chinese officials for the drowning of a Chinese woman, although her death seems to have been accidental. After resisting the demands of the Chinese authorities as long as they dared, the Americans were finally required to surrender the accused, who was promptly tried and executed (October, 1821).

demanded less restricted trading facilities, the opening of ports other than Canton and the abrogation of the monopolistic privileges of the *co-hong*.[15] Furthermore, they were exasperated by the Chinese tariff duties, which varied with the whims of officials. To these sources of discontent must be added the insistence of the British for equal diplomatic intercourse and for Western justice in China. Such were the factors that laid the fire. The match was supplied by the trade in opium. While it is probably true that war was inevitable between an arrogantly exclusive China and an aggressive, industrial Britain, it is equally true that the immediate cause of conflict was the Chinese attempt to exterminate the traffic in a baneful drug.

The greater part of the opium supply shipped to China came from two sources, the Ganges valley of British India and the native states of Central India. Over the first area of production the East India Company in the latter part of the eighteenth century had declared a monopoly, while over the other source it exercised a measure of control. The Company itself did not import opium into China, but its product was sold in Calcutta to private merchants who transported it to Canton and disposed of it there.[16] During the early part of the nineteenth century imports rose

---

[15] The *co-hong* was opposed partly because its monopolistic position unnecessarily restricted the operations of Western merchants and partly because, under the intolerable weight of official exactions, its members developed a distressing tendency toward bankruptcy.

[16] The only important exception to this statement is the voyage of two vessels which carried opium to China on the Company's account. This episode occurred in 1781-82 during the governorship of Warren Hastings.

steadily until in the year 1837-38 more than twenty-eight thousand chests entered China.[17]

The policy of the Chinese government toward this unsavory trade is full of apparent paradoxes. Years before the question became acute, opium had been declared contraband by the emperor. His reasons seem to have been purely those of morality. Unfortunately, the administration at Canton, in whose hands rested the enforcement of the prohibitory edicts was much less implacable in its prejudices against the drug, or at any rate, such prejudices as it possessed were usually sacrificed in the interests of "squeeze."[18] The result was that, with the complaisance of officialdom, the opium trade was carried on at Canton openly and, in the main, steadily. During the third decade of the century, ethical arguments were reënforced by financial considerations, when the emperor and his advisers concluded that the opium traffic had altered the balance of trade with the West and that the specie resources of the Middle Kingdom were being drained away as payment for a narcotic poison.[19] Thereupon the emperor resolved

[17] A chest of Bengal opium contained 133⅓ pounds.

[18] The regular salary of a Chinese official was utterly incommensurate with his expenses. Consequently, the bureaucracy was honeycombed with graft, or as it is commonly known among foreigners in China, "squeeze." The Peking government was relatively impotent to prevent corruption because of the decentralization of the entire system.

[19] The general trade between Europe and China had produced a balance overwhelmingly in favor of China, since the market for European goods was a highly restricted one. Consequently, there had been a steady movement of silver toward the Far East. But if British woolens were given short shrift by the Chinese, their prejudices by no means extended to Indian opium. Foreign merchants thus discovered a way of righting the unfavorable balance by importing opium from India. This fact helps to account for the extraordinary expansion of the drug trade during the early nineteenth century.

upon heroic action as the only means of suppressing the opium traffic.

THE FIRST WAR WITH GREAT BRITAIN

The person selected to carry out the imperial mandate was one Lin Tse-sü, who was sent to Canton in the spring of 1839. His program of direct, vigorous action seemed incredible to the foreigners, accustomed to the devious paths pursued by most Chinese officials of their acquaintance. After imprisoning the foreign merchants in their factories for some days, he succeeded in confiscating some twenty thousand chests of opium, which he duly destroyed. To sincere, if somewhat narrow, Chinese such as Lin, the case was transparently clear. Foreigners had abused the privilege that China had extended to them by dealing in a contraband drug. There was but one issue at stake between Great Britain and China, and that issue was opium. To the British the matter was scarcely less plain. They had no intention of forcing China to accept opium, but the action of Commissioner Lin was regarded as a national affront as well as a wanton destruction of property. Furthermore, now that a *casus belli* had arisen, the time was ripe for redressing the perennial grievances of British subjects in China and obtaining a more favorable status for British mercantile interests. Thus from the British point of view, the coming war was to force open the gates of China, not to impose opium upon her.

As a result of the somewhat tactless vigor of Commissioner Lin, then, there was created a situation which made war almost unavoidable. It was a sadly unequal conflict, for the forces of the Chinese, although large, were equipped with the most primitive weapons. Only a small minority possessed firearms of any sort, while, on the water, the war junks of the Chinese were ridiculous when pitted against the ships of the greatest naval power in the world. The British devoted themselves to capturing the principal seaports of south and central China and then sailed up the Yangtse to Nanking, where the Chinese, rendered desperate by the futility of their arms, sued for peace.

THE TREATY OF NANKING

The stakes of the war, as interpreted by Great Britain, are clearly reflected in the treaty of Nanking (1842). Opium was left utterly unmentioned, save that an indemnity was required for the quantity destroyed by the zealous Lin. The real objective of the treaty, as of the war, was to obtain security and improved commercial opportunities for British nationals in China. The principal terms of the treaty may be summarized briefly. Five ports, including Canton, were to be opened to the trade and residence of British subjects. An indemnity of some twenty-one million dollars was to be paid by China for the opium confiscated, for the expenses of the British expeditionary force, and for debts contracted by the *hong* merchants. Uniform tariff rates were to be imposed and the *co-hong* abolished. The tariff duties, as they were established in the following year, were generally based on the low rate of five per cent *ad valorem*. The island of Hongkong was ceded outright to Great Britain. Finally, British officials were to communicate with Chinese authorities on equal terms. This provision involved the recognition of consular officers, but not, as yet, of ministers who would reside at the Chinese capital.

In the following year a supplementary treaty with Great Britain was signed, which contained one clause of far-reaching significance. This first statement of the "most-favored-nation" doctrine provided, in a word, that the status enjoyed by British subjects in China should be in nowise inferior to that of citizens of any other state. Commercial privileges extended, for example, to Americans, must apply also to the British. This clause, written by other powers into their treaties with China, virtually guaranteed equal rights and privileges to all foreigners. Its embodiment in the British treaty of 1843 again emphasizes the fact that neither Great Britain nor any other nation was seeking exclusive rights in China, nor were they trying to enlarge their imperial possessions. It was trade and security for traders that drove the British to storm the walls of China.

THE AMERICAN TREATY

The armed forces and diplomatists of Great Britain fought the battle that brought China to her knees, but other countries were not slow to take advantage of the new opportunities. In no nation of the West had the treaty of Nanking created more of a sensation than in the American republic, whose trade with the Far East had undergone an amazing expansion and whose merchants were not to be denied the fruits of Britain's successful war. Caleb Cushing was therefore commissioned to negotiate with the partially humbled China

The treaty with which he returned obtained for Americans all that the British had wrested and more.[20] The most important clause of the Cushing treaty was that dealing with extra-territoriality. As we have seen, Western experience with Chinese justice had been long and painful, and the only method of avoiding conflict appeared to be the application of a plan similar to that which had obtained for centuries in the Levant. Shorn of much complexity, extra-territoriality is the right of an alien who appears as the defendant in a case to be tried under his national code of laws administered by his consul. An agreement supplementary to the British treaty of Nanking included an article which provided somewhat vaguely for extra-territoriality in criminal cases. Cushing both defined the right more precisely and extended it to include civil cases as well.[21]

In her first important treaties with the West, China thus lost not only control over her tariff arrangements but jurisdiction over those who lived within her boundaries. Although at the time extra-territoriality appeared the only way out of an irreconcilable conflict, yet it has been a serious infraction of China's sovereignty. In the treaty ports there have been erected foreign settlements which owe allegiance not to Peking but to Washington, Paris, and London. These settlements or "concessions" are administered by Western

[20] In certain respects, the policy of the American negotiator differed from that of the British plenipotentiaries. Opium, for example, was definitely conceded to be contraband, and the United States pledged herself to take measures against her citizens engaged in the traffic. It may be said at once that this clause promptly became a dead letter, and American as well as British merchants continued to ply their illegal trade.

[21] Treaties were also negotiated by France in 1844 and by Sweden and Norway in 1847.

officials in accordance with Western law. It is scarcely a matter for surprise that the abolition of extra-territoriality represents one of the major demands of the new nationalist government of China.

The Middle Kingdom had thus been brought into official relations with the West and had made the best terms it could. Although China had by no means accepted membership in the community of nations, Western influences began to play upon her and imperceptibly to alter the attitudes of a few of her citizens. Henceforth, the historical evolution of the Chinese state was conditioned by the new factors. Despite the ultimate significance of the treaties, at the time they produced little more than a precarious equilibrium, unsatisfactory to the Chinese and soon to become so to foreigners. They had created a state of affairs which would lead inexorably to further assaults upon Chinese isolation. Another war was necessary to define the relationship of the two civilizations.

CHAPTER II

THE CHANGING ORIENT, 1844-1901

DURING the years between 1844 and 1901 the waves of profound change swept over the Far East. From the flood emerged a new China and a new Japan. In 1844 neither had been appreciably affected by the West, and for China, especially, the process of accommodation was to be long and painful. The concessions granted to foreigners by the reluctant Middle Kingdom after the Anglo-Chinese war were at best halfway measures inevitably to be extended under further pressure from the West. It was inconceivable that European nations, always avid for commerce, would be satisfied with the grudging tolerance that the Chinese now accorded them. The assault was to continue until the barriers against the West had been beaten down. China, once the haughtiest of nations, was to find herself humiliated and prostrate before the industrialized and militarized West, the stake of competitive imperialisms.

Japan, in 1844, was even less open to foreign influence than was her continental neighbor. Indeed, no serious attempts had been made against her isolation. But during the second half of the nineteenth century, she experienced an extraordinary metamorphosis. With almost lightning speed she reorganized her entire political system, while equally significant changes followed in the fields of industry, commerce, and education.

THE SECOND ANGLO-CHINESE WAR

For China the period between the Opium war and that with Japan (1894) was characterized by growing, if unsought, intimacy with the West. The two civilizations were finding new points of contact which too often became new points of friction. It soon appeared that the treaties of Nanking had done little or nothing to abate the anti-foreign prejudice of Chinese officialdom. The authorities displayed little desire to put the terms of the treaty into execution, and at Canton a series of anti-foreign demonstrations occurred, in some instances with ample provocation. Foreign merchants, on the other hand, found that even the new freedom was not enough. They were eager to vend the products of British industry to the millions in the interior, to see additional ports opened to trade, and to navigate the principal rivers of the country. Missionaries desired general toleration for Christianity and freedom to spread their religion inland.[1]

The essential cause of the second Anglo-Chinese war was the dissatisfaction of foreign merchants with the treatment that they had received since 1844. Indeed, the British government had determined to press for a revision of the treaties, even before another war came within the range of immediate possibility. With such a policy already decided upon, it required only the indiscretion of an over-zealous Chinese official to provide the occasion. In October, 1856, a party of Chinese

[1] In 1844-45 the emperor had issued edicts of toleration for both Catholics and Protestants. This concession, however, did not give missionaries the right to carry on their work outside the treaty ports.

soldiery boarded the *lorcha Arrow* [2] and arrested the Chinese crew on a charge of piracy. To the demand of the British consul for an apology and the surrender of the crew, the Chinese officials granted the latter but denied the former. The scene was again laid for violent action. A British admiral stationed in Chinese waters immediately captured the forts around Canton. When word of the outrage reached England, the government saw in the conflict, which had already become a fact, an admirable wedge for the further opening of China and for a favorable revision of the treaties of 1842-44. Once more the British "taxpayer contributed that the merchants and manufacturers might benefit."

The details of the second Anglo-Chinese war (1856-60) are neither interesting nor important. In her armed protest Great Britain was joined by France, eager to enforce a revision of the treaties but professedly acting to obtain redress for the murder of a French missionary.[3] After a period of operations in the Canton area, the allies determined to press north, where they could deal more effectively with the intransigent court. The forts at the mouth of the Peiho river were taken without difficulty, and the European army advanced to Tientsin, the seaport of Peking. There the British and French envoys, accompanied

[2] *Lorcha* was the name applied to vessels whose hulls were similar to Western ships but which were rigged like Chinese junks. They were frequently engaged in the more unsavory varieties of eastern trade, such as that in opium. For a discussion of the legal status of the *Arrow*, see Morse, *International Relations of the Chinese Empire*, I, pp. 423-425.

[3] It should be pointed out that the missionary, Père Chapdelaine, had gone into Kwangsi province, far from any treaty port. Thus his trial and execution constituted no real infraction of the French treaty.

by plenipotentiaries from Russia and the United States, in June, 1858, negotiated the treaties of Tientsin. These new engagements registered the demands of the commercial community in that they provided for the opening of five new ports and for a revision of the tariff. Toleration was granted to the Christian religion throughout the empire, and foreigners were to be allowed to travel in the interior. Finally, ministers from foreign powers were to be permitted to reside in Peking and to negotiate with officials of the central government of China.

The Chinese government, however, had not yet capitulated. When the foreign envoys started for Peking, where ratifications were to be exchanged, they found their way again blocked by the forts on the Peiho. The foreign envoys were convinced that they must not yield to Chinese obstinacy and bad faith but must press on to Peking where they could deal with the central government itself. The result was a joint Anglo-French expedition which captured Tientsin and, in the autumn of 1860, occupied the Manchu capital.

The treaties of Tientsin definitely and finally altered the balance of power between China and the West. Hitherto it had been the Middle Kingdom which had prescribed the conditions of international intercourse and had laid down regulations for the barbarians. Henceforth, after a display of power that was convincing even to the parochial Chinese, it was the West that was to dictate terms. The real opening of China was accomplished by the second war, to which the first had been but a preliminary. There was still much to be done, but Chinese isolation had now become a matter of history.

China's resistance to the allied arms was vitiated by internal conflict. Sporadic rebellions broke out, and one of them, the Taiping, seriously threatened the throne itself. This uprising (1851-64) began as a religious movement, the result of Christianity imperfectly comprehended, but, as a result of persecution by the government, it was transformed into an antidynastic rebellion. Gathering strength as they moved northward, the rebels captured Nanking and threatened the Manchu capital. The Taiping program, especially in its later phases, was purely destructive, and the insurgents succeeded in alienating both Chinese and foreigners. It was only through the aid of the latter that the uprising was suppressed, but not until central China had been thoroughly devastated, the internal administration thrown into chaos, and the Peking government embarrassed in dealing with Western powers.[4]

Indeed, the latter half of the nineteenth century gave indubitable evidence of the approaching collapse of the Manchu dynasty. The power of the emperors,

---

[4] The Taiping rebellion gave rise to a very curious but useful institution, the foreign-administered customs service. When Shanghai fell into the hands of a group of rebels, the native customs service was unable to continue. The foreign community appointed a board to see to the collection of duties. This system proved so satisfactory that it was finally developed into a regular customs service and applied to other treaty ports. In this way it completely superseded the old form of collection by native functionaries. In the new service the more responsible positions are held by foreigners, but they are employees of the Chinese government.

most of them children and all incompetents, was plainly declining, and the palace eunuchs were gaining influence, an almost infallible sign of decay in a Chinese dynasty. The rulers were dominated by an extraordinary woman, the Empress Dowager Tz'u Hsi, whose secluded life had left her ignorant and narrow, but whose great ability supported the tottering dynasty beyond its natural span of life.

THE BEGINNINGS OF WESTERNIZATION, 1860-94

Quite naturally, the treaties of Tientsin, with the more favorable status which they conceded to foreigners in China, multiplied the contacts, both official and unofficial, between the two civilizations. At the behest of the powers a foreign office, the Tsung-li Yamen, was created to deal with the ministers from abroad, and, although the officials of the new bureau were by no means enthusiastic over their relations with Western diplomatists, they gradually became somewhat less fearsome. In the late sixties, they were persuaded by foreigners who believed that the modernization of China was imminent, to send a commission to Europe and America. Tentative beginnings were also made in the field of education and in the construction of telegraph lines and railroads. But China was not prepared to westernize herself as rapidly as the more visionary foreigners believed that she might. As a Chinese official observed, "The only instruction we gave our envoy [at the time of the mission mentioned above] was to keep the West from forcing us to build railways and telegraphs, which we want only so far as they are due to our own initiative." The vast lump of conservatism had been scarcely leavened, and only a few of the Chinese leaders sought to push their country haltingly toward reform.

CHRISTIAN MISSIONS IN CHINA

Another foreign influence brought to bear upon China was that of an ever-increasing body of missionaries from the West. In the old China, propagandists of Christianity were not wholly unknown, for Franciscans had visited the empire in the thirteenth and fourteenth centuries. The Jesuits, who followed the Portuguese seamen to the Orient, were hospitably received at court until their unseemly conflict with the other missionaries over such questions as ancestor-worship and the interference of the Papacy in what were regarded as purely Chinese questions led to their interdiction in 1707.[5] At this time, there were perhaps three hundred thousand native Christians in China. Thereafter, until the arms of the West forced toleration for Christianity, the Chinese officially would have nothing to do with exotic religions, despite their usual indulgence in such matters.

The first Protestant missionary, who reached China in 1807, was obliged to smuggle himself into the country, so strict was the Chinese prohibition of religious propaganda. The Chinese official might tolerate traders for the profit which they brought, but he had no desire to see other foreigners add themselves to the commercial community. During pre-treaty days, therefore, missionaries found their freedom, if any-

[5] The edict of 1707 did not constitute an actual prohibition, but it marked the beginning of a long period of intense persecution.

thing, more seriously curtailed than was that of the merchants. The treaties of 1842-44, although giving the representatives of Western Christianity something less than they had hoped for, were of some importance in that they opened four new ports to their residence. Moreover, in 1844, the emperor, at the request of France, had agreed to tolerate Catholicism, and in the following year, he extended the same favor to Protestantism.

Between the two wars (1842-1856), missionary interest in China increased immensely, the number of Protestant missionaries being more than doubled. At the same time, the disabilities under which they labored appeared the more impressive as the West grew more concerned over the religious welfare of the Chinese. When the treaties following the second war were negotiated, the missionaries were able to press their claims with great vigor. Indeed, they occupied a peculiarly strategic position, especially in connection with the American treaty, for two scholarly members of the missionary body acted as secretaries to the plenipotentiary, and, because of their command of the language, they carried on most of the actual discussion. It was one of these secretaries who drafted the rather vague article which conferred toleration upon Christians in China. The French treaty contained a still more far-reaching provision, when it obliged the Chinese government to protect missionaries going into the interior.

The half century after these concessions had been obtained was a period of rich growth for Christian missions in China. By 1890 there were some half million of Chinese Catholics and about fifty-five thousand Protestants, while the number of Protestant missionaries had increased from seventy-five in 1856 to nearly thirteen hundred in 1889. Along with this numerical expansion went augmented emphasis upon medical and educational work. The doctor appeared early in the history of Protestant missions, and the record of mission hospitals and medical schools in China has been a distinguished one. In addition to the elementary schools of the earlier days, secondary schools and colleges were now established. Such institutions have offered, by and large, the best training in Western studies to be had in China. Missionaries thus became the principal emissaries of science and education, and consequently, as the current of westernization gained momentum among the Chinese, early hostility gave way to cordiality. Notwithstanding whatever criticisms may be directed against Christian missions, it is probably fair to say that they helped to prepare China for a transition that was inevitable, although painful, and that they have revealed to the Chinese a side of Western life which the typical "treaty-port foreigner" only rarely reflects.

THE ISOLATION OF JAPAN

When European seamen first approached the island kingdom in the days of the discoveries, the door had not yet been closed against foreigners. In the middle of the sixteenth century came Portuguese traders and Portuguese Jesuits, and early in the following century they were reënforced by merchants representing the Dutch and English East India Companies. Although the Japanese government was far from cordial toward these ambassadors from the West, they met with moderately indulgent treatment. But unholy bickerings between the religious orders, international jealousies of the traders, and the political danger implicit in Jesuit propaganda caused the rulers of Japan to take thought. A series of edicts was therefore promulgated which proscribed Christianity and ordered the missionaries deported (1587-1612). Those who returned were persecuted in a bloodthirsty fashion. So deeply did these episodes impress themselves upon foreigners that, as late as 1799, a vessel going to Japan was supplied with the following instructions:

"All the books of the people and officers, particularly religious books, must be put in a cask and headed up [upon approaching Japan]; the officers from shore will put their seals upon the cask, and take it on shore, and on the departure of the ship will bring it on board without having opened it."

The antipathy of the Japanese toward the Jesuits was soon reflected in their attitude toward Portuguese and Spanish merchants, who could not dissociate themselves from the Christian propaganda of their countrymen. The rulers of Japan during this period made it their policy to encourage commerce, and they would have welcomed trade relations, if the latter could have been divorced from religious and political complications. They were convinced, however, that all Spaniards and Portuguese, missionary and trader alike, must go. The shogun was confirmed in his decision by a "Christian" revolt (1638), responsibility for which was ascribed to the Portuguese. Japan thereupon proceeded to isolate herself. It had already been decreed that no native was to leave the islands, and now the defiant challenge was thrown out to the European world, "So long as the sun warms the earth, any Christian so bold as to come to Japan, even if he be King Philip of Spain himself or the God of the Christians, shall pay for it with his head." [6]

Henceforth the policy of Japan was definitely anti-foreign, though perhaps not quite as virulently so as one might gather from the foregoing. When the shogun said "Christian" he meant "Roman Catholic." Toward Protestants his antipathies were somewhat less violent, especially if they preserved a decent reticence with respect to their religious views. The Dutch were allowed to remain at Nagasaki, subject to regulations far more restrictive than those we have already observed at Canton. The English had voluntarily abandoned their factory in Japan, and when, later in the century, they asked to be readmitted, permission was refused on the ground that the English king, Charles II, had married a Portuguese princess. For the Japanese were singularly lukewarm toward anything connected even remotely with Portugal.

THE OPENING OF JAPAN

During the early nineteenth century Japan managed to preserve her isolation almost unimpaired. Yet she was not without premonitions that attempts might be made against her exclusive policy, now two centuries old. Japanese seclusion was not so complete but that

---

[6] This quotation is perhaps apocryphal, but it expresses with sufficient accuracy the attitude of the Japanese government.

her statesmen could read the signs of the times. They viewed with apprehension the advance of Russia into the northern island of the archipelago; they remarked the aggressive West humiliating their neighbor, China; they had seen the British possess themselves of much of the Indian peninsula; and they determined that Japan should not share the fate of other Oriental peoples.

The decisive assault upon Japanese isolation came from the United States. Although the forces which produced the pressure of the West upon Japan were much the same as those which bore on China, other circumstances dictated that the United States rather than Great Britain should play the most important rôle. Since the Revolution land hunger had driven American settlers inexorably westward. By mid-century the covered-wagon pioneers had occupied the Oregon country, and their hold on the Pacific coast was reënforced by the gold rush to California. The creation of a flourishing American colony in the Far West meant an expansion of American commercial interests across the Pacific. Such interests were not to be satisfied by the traditional Japanese policy. For example, there was the question of shipwrecked sailors. Disasters to whaling craft in the uncharted waters of Japan were only too common, and seamen cast ashore suffered great hardship and brutality. Plans for steam navigation in the Pacific raised the problem of coaling stations. Altogether it seemed imperative to the American government that Japan should be persuaded to depart from her traditional policy of exclusion.

THE PERRY EXPEDITION

These objectives are clearly set forth in the instructions issued to Commodore Perry in 1852. The expedition which he was to lead was enjoined to obtain three concessions from the Japanese government: better treatment for shipwrecked sailors, the privilege of purchasing coal, and the opening of at least one port to American trade. It may be said at once that Japan, as well as China, was opened by Western force, although the force was held in reserve and never actually drawn upon. The commodore was ordered to use pacific methods, but if the Japanese proved unduly obdurate, he was to "change his tone" and to assure the islanders that his government would protect its citizens at all costs. "No friendship," insisted the president's letter to the emperor, "can long exist between them [the president and the emperor] unless Japan should change her policy and cease to act towards the people of the United States as if they were her enemies."

In the summer of 1853 Perry's four ships cast anchor in Araga Bay, near Tokyo, and remained there for more than a week. The Japanese proved obstinate and the commodore's diplomacy became brusque. After much urging, the officials finally agreed to transmit President Fillmore's letter to their emperor. After he had seen his message safely on its way to the capital, Perry withdrew the fleet, promising to return in the spring for an answer to his demands.

THE TREATY OF PEACE AND AMITY

By the time the American vessels reappeared the Japanese had determined to capitulate. To a sufficient number of leaders, resistance to Perry's demands seemed a suicidal course, one that had led the Chinese only to disaster. Consequently the negotiations proceeded with unexpected placidity. The terms of the new treaty dealt rather leniently with Japan. Indeed, the West got no more than an opening wedge. Shipwrecked sailors were to be treated more courteously, and Americans were permitted to trade at Nagasaki and two smaller ports, but under a mass of restrictions. Similar provisions were also written into treaties with Great Britain, Russia, and the Netherlands.

It was the achievement of Townsend Harris, the first American consul-general to Japan, to bring Perry's work to fruition. Circumstances lent persuasiveness to the arguments of the tactful American, who, unaided by the force of gunboats, persuaded the Japanese leaders to enter into relations with the West. He pointed convincingly to the second Anglo-Chinese war, which was demonstrating the folly of resistance. Largely as a result of the confidence which the Japanese reposed in Harris, they voluntarily proceeded to the negotiation of a new treaty (1858). Its terms were rather similar to those of the treaty of Tientsin. Additional ports were to be opened to trade, with foreign consuls in residence and a diplomatic agent stationed at the capital. Religious toleration was extended to Americans in Japan, although the Japanese refused to grant this concession to their own subjects. Americans were to enjoy extra-territorial privileges and the benefits of tariff duties arranged by treaty. On the whole, the Townsend Harris agreement was a triumph for peaceful diplomacy.

THE WESTERNIZATION OF JAPAN

The immediate effect of this sudden forcing of the doors was to throw the internal politics of Japan into chaos. There were wide differences of opinion within the country. Should the Japanese unite to repel the rude invaders? Should they open the door only as far as demanded by the peremptory powers? Or should they welcome the foreigner, learn all that he had to teach, and ultimately be in a position to compete with him on his own terms? Those who held the last opinion, at the outset an inconsiderable minority, were within fifteen years to become the dominant group and to lead in the phenomenal transformation of the Japanese state.

The political situation in Japan in 1858 was a complex one. The country, it will be recalled, was actually governed by a military leader, the shogun, who was the foremost feudal chieftain. The emperor, in whom supreme authority was nominally vested, was but a symbol. The state was still feudalized, and the barons, whose turbulence varied inversely with the strength of the shogunate, were in practise governors of their respective localities. During the eighteenth century a restoration movement had been gaining force, a movement which contemplated the abolition of the shogunate and the recognition of the emperor as sovereign in fact as well as in name. The currents which produced the restoration party were of many kinds. On the one hand, were the researches of Japanese historians, who convinced themselves that the emperor was the rightful ruler, and the agitation for a revival of Shinto as the national religion, for emperor-worship was its most characteristic feature. On the other hand, there were the hard political facts. The Tokugawa family, hereditary shoguns, was palpably declining, while the larger feudal lords were usurping whatever power they could lay their hands upon. In short, the assault of the West coincided with a crucial situation in Japanese domestic politics.

Nevertheless, it was the pressure of the West that precipitated the crisis. By many, especially those of the restoration party, the shogun's cooperation with foreigners was regarded as a weakness. "Exalt the Emperor! Away with the barbarians!" was the rallying cry of the opponents of the shogun. Strangely enough, the exclusionists, bent on restoring the emperor and expelling the foreigners, were later to become the most active of reformers. But for the present their chief aim was to embarrass the shogun, already hopelessly beset by internal difficulties and foreign demands. Because of his inept handling of crises with foreigners, the powers in 1867 jointly demanded the resignation of the shogun. The latter readily complied, for, in all probability, he was not averse to passing from the scene as gracefully as possible.

THE BEGINNINGS OF REFORM

Fortunately for the West, the restoration party now executed an amazing reversal in its policy. One might have expected that the demands of the powers would have played into the hands of the most virulently anti-foreign party in the state. Just as the shogunate was being abolished, however, the old emperor, one of the most violent of exclusionists, died and was succeeded by Meiji (1867-1912), who soon revealed himself, in spite of his youth, as one determined to lead his people along the difficult but inevitable path of westernization.

Around the standard of the emperor thus gathered all those who felt that the crisis demanded nothing less than thorough reorganization. Obviously the first change to be made was to transform the structure of the state from a group of powerful fiefs into a modern, centralized government. As long as feudal chieftains enjoyed semi-independent jurisdiction, any central administration would be largely farcical. But the situation required caution, and the government therefore proceeded to the execution of its policy with the greatest care. The first step was to appoint an imperial official for each fief, after which regulations were promulgated for the uniform government of all fiefs and for the limitation of private armies. Then occurred a most spectacular event. With little warning, four of the greatest military chieftains of the islands offered to relinquish their feudal rights. Their example was followed by nearly 250 other lords. Here was the manifesto of Japanese barons that they were ready to aid in the work of reorganization. In no nation of Europe was the transition from feudalism to nationalism accomplished so smoothly as in this Oriental state.

POLITICAL RECONSTRUCTION

The abolition of feudalism had done little more than to clear the ground for positive reconstruction. Other problems faced the leaders of the awakened Japan. A governmental organization must be substituted for the discredited feudal system; the authority of the emperor must be made supreme in fact as well as in name. The military and naval forces of the state must be remodeled, and the financial system modernized. To make the task still more staggering, all of these reforms must be carried through in the face of a public opinion at times violently hostile, at others merely inert.

Even before the fight to rid the country of feudal particularism, constructive measures were already under way. The central government had been organized in seven departments, with prefects in charge of local administration. These prefects met each year at the capital, and a sort of privy council nominated by the government also gave what advice was desired. Neither of these bodies enjoyed real parliamentary power.

To absorb feudalism on paper, the government soon perceived, was a much simpler matter than to do it in reality. One of the most crying needs was to demolish the stratified social structure of the old order, to reduce the status of the *samurai* and to raise that of the commoners. Although the *samurai* had lost their political preeminence, they still expected to dominate the military system as they had done in the past. The government was rightly convinced that this must not be and that the army of the new Japan must be a national institution. A decree issued late in 1871 established universal military service, so that the defense of the state became the obligation of every citizen. When, five years later, the *samurai* were denied their immemorial privilege of wearing swords, the knightly class was assimilated into the citizenry, and all Japanese subjects occupied the same legal status.[7]

In general, the *samurai* accepted their lot with the stoical resignation which had been bred into them through the centuries. Nevertheless, there were many whose eyes turned wistfully back to the days when they had been the privileged class. Partly in opposition to what they regarded as an unnecessarily pacific policy in dealing with Korea and partly in an attempt to regain their old military position, the *samurai* in one of the large fiefs (Satsuma) rose in revolt. The civil war was bitterly contested, but within a few months the new national army had proved its superiority. In September, 1877, the rebels laid down their arms. This episode represented the last important protest of the old Japan.

AGITATION FOR REPRESENTATIVE INSTITUTIONS

Before the centralizing process had been completed, there arose the demand for representative government. Hitherto, the affairs of state had been in the hands of the emperor and his ministers, who, in general, represented the most important of the clans and tended to become an oligarchy. The movement for constitutional government drew its strength both from political malcontents and from genuine liberals, and, indeed, members of the government seem to have resisted the pressure chiefly because of their feeling that the change

---

[7] The Japanese social hierarchy included, first of course, the military *samurai,* then farmers, artisans, merchants, and, finally, a class called the *eta,* who were condemned, by heredity, to perform the most menial tasks of the community. Obviously, official decrees might alter the position of the *samurai,* but only long years of education can swing the *eta* from his traditional groove.

would be premature. In 1881 the conservatives surrendered, announcing that a national assembly would be summoned in 1890 and that a constitution would be promulgated.

Prince Ito was immediately sent abroad to study political methods in the West. Upon his return the work of framing a constitution was promptly begun by a commission of which he was the head. Ito had discovered in Prussia a government with whose system and traditions he felt those of Japan to be most nearly in harmony, and he incorporated many of these ideas in the system that he was creating. In order to prepare the nation for the new constitution, he created a new nobility which would supply the members of the upper house of the legislature, and he reorganized the cabinet upon the pattern of the German body. By 1889 the new constitution was ready, and with the sanction of the emperor it was put into operation.

THE GOVERNMENTAL STRUCTURE OF JAPAN

Ito's constitution was by no means a radical instrument of government. Following closely its German prototype, it assigns to the emperor a cardinal place in the new system. He embodies all sovereignty. He orders the foreign relations of his state, is commander-in-chief of the army and navy, and appoints and controls members of the bureaucracy. Yet in reality, for all his exalted position, the emperor of Japan has much less to do with the government than had the German kaiser.

The legislative assembly or Imperial Diet is bicameral, composed of a house of peers and a house of representatives. The upper house includes members of the nobility, imperial nominees, and a few of the higher taxpayers. Since 1925 members of the house of representatives have been elected by universal manhood suffrage. The Diet must assent to all laws, but its measures are subject to the absolute veto of the emperor. There is no generic connection between the Diet and the cabinet, which remains the servant of the emperor rather than of the legislature.[8] But, practically speaking, it is very difficult for a government to survive unless it controls a majority in the lower house.

The constitution also recognized the existence of a Privy Council, which had been established earlier. This body bears an advisory relation to the emperor, and its members are appointed by him. In addition to these three bodies, there was a fourth, unprovided for in the constitution and peculiar to Japan,—the "elder statesmen" (*Genro*). This group of men, leaders in the westernization movement in the 70's and 80's, became one of the most influential factors in the Japanese state. At times of crisis, their unofficial opinion frequently was given precedence over that of cabinet and council. With the death of its original members, this extraordinary institution ceased to exist.

THE ECONOMIC REVOLUTION

Parallel with the transformation of the political structure went changes no less significant in the field of economic life. When Commodore Perry appeared

---

[8] A partial exception to this statement is to be found in the right of interpellation. Ministers may be questioned in regard to their policies on the floor of the Diet.

in Araga Bay, Japan was living under a medieval system of economy. Agriculture was the predominant means of livelihood. There was almost no mobile capital, and trade had failed to reach the proportions that it had achieved in China. One of the most immediate necessities was a less archaic method of communication. At first, the Japanese showed no great desire to adopt the telegraph or the railroad. They had all of the Oriental's contentment with leisurely modes of travel. It was a rice famine in the southern part of the island that first turned the eyes of Japanese leaders to the need for better transportation facilities. In 1870 the Tokyo-Yokohama line was begun, and two years later it was opened by the emperor himself. The government had taken the lead in the project, and had carried it through against the most violent opposition from the champions of the old order. At about the same time a start was made in the construction of telegraph lines.

The manufacturing industries of the Old Japan had been, of course, the domain of the handicraftsman. In the days of feudalism, the work of the armorers, for example, had reached a high standard of perfection, and later, when the interests of the barons were less restricted to warfare, their courts encouraged a wide variety of crafts. When contact with the West revealed a civilization infinitely superior in quantity production, Japanese leaders coveted the new industrialism for their people. How could it be introduced? The islanders were utterly unfamiliar with the mechanism of industry in both its technical and financial aspects. The government solved the problem by itself entering the industrial field as the instructor of its people. To stimulate the old handicrafts, a firm was created by the government to advertise the work of Japanese artisans in foreign markets. Japan, indeed, absorbed the new technique so rapidly that, whereas in 1871 there were no large-scale industries on the islands, by 1896 there were more than four thousand companies, with a paid-up capital of nearly two hundred millions of dollars. Incidentally, it may be pointed out that this economic transformation left in its wake a set of social problems already familiar to those who have followed the course of the industrial revolution in the West.

CULTURAL CHANGES

Like her political and economic systems, the culture of Japan was profoundly altered by association with the West. In no sphere was the appropriation of foreign ideas more avid than in that of education. Whatever the merit of the old Japanese education, the new order obviously required a different training. The government became convinced that nothing less than education for both leaders and masses would enable the country to build on a secure foundation. The far-reaching objectives which the Japanese statesmen sought to achieve may be gathered from the educational law of 1872: "All people, high or low, and of both sexes, should receive education, so that there should not be found one family in the whole empire, nor one member of a family, ignorant and illiterate." Immediate steps were taken to realize this ideal. Elementary schools were established in large numbers so that as early as 1874 about one-third of the children of school age were receiving instruction.[9]

To-day there are four imperial universities in the country, in addition to technical, medical, and agricultural schools. Below these institutions of higher grade, normal, secondary, and primary schools reach the rank and file of the citizenry. Besides the state system, there have been established many private institutions, under both religious and secular auspices. Such, for example, are the Universities of Waseda and Keio, known to American undergraduates chiefly by the baseball teams which they occasionally send to this country. The former was founded by Marquis Okuma, one of the most gifted of the "Elder Statesmen."

More important perhaps than the formal education offered by the new system was the intellectual leaven working throughout all of Japanese life. Numbers of young men had received their training in the universities of the West and they began to wield a powerful influence. A veritable crop of newspapers sprang up, holding various shades of opinion, which many of them advocated with offensive blatancy. Western literature was translated into Japanese. Foreigners were employed by the government to interpret the ways and customs of the West. In short, the entire pattern of Japanese life was being altered.

[9] In 1923 the percentage of illiteracy was less than one per cent. This forms a striking contrast to conditions prevailing in China, where, according to an estimate of the Chinese National Association of the Mass Education Movement, only about twenty per cent of the population could be considered literate. *World Almanac,* 1929, pp. 734-35.

CHRISTIANITY IN THE CHANGING JAPAN

Another foreign influence brought to bear upon Japan in the days of change was that supplied by missionaries. From the eviction of the Jesuits in the seventeenth century to the Harris treaty of 1858 the islands were tightly closed against all Christian propaganda. When once the doors were opened, American churches promptly sent their representatives. During the 70's and 80's, when worship of things Western became almost an article in the creed of patriotic Japanese, the Christian community grew with incredible rapidity. It was an age of transition and anything new was eagerly seized upon. Then came the inevitable nationalist reaction against the leadership which foreigners had assumed in Japanese life, and the prospects for the early conversion of the islanders became much less favorable.

The outstanding characteristic of missionary activity in Japan, however, is not the size of the Christian church, which is by no means imposing, but rather the influence which it exerts, out of all proportion to its numerical strength. The fact that the state itself had determined upon a course of reform led many of its leaders to the Western religion, so that almost from the first the church was the property of the Japanese rather than of the foreign missionaries. Many of the early missionaries, too, showed great tact and ability in their efforts to aid the Japanese in their stupendous task of reorganization. Verbeck, the first Protestant missionary to enter the country, was invited to aid in developing educational policy, and for the better part of a decade he took a large part in directing the new system. Others were accepted as trusted advisers of the Japanese government.

FOREIGN POLICY

It was not merely the internal structure of the Japanese state that was made over to conform to Western forms. The new-born national spirit also expressed itself in a vigorous assertion of equality with other nations. The Japanese were keenly sensible of the international disabilities under which they had been placed. Treaty relations with the West had robbed them both of tariff autonomy and of judicial control of foreign residents, for the extra-territorial system, it will be recalled, had been applied to Japan as well as to China.[10] As early as 1871 Japanese statesmen were seeking to convince the West that such limitations of sovereignty were no longer appropriate, but their efforts, for the time being, proved unavailing. Meanwhile, to prepare for the abolition of the odious extra-territoriality, the courts were entirely reorganized, and law schools established. Once again, Japan demanded that foreigners relinquish their special privileges, and, after a long period of negotiation, the West capitulated. In 1894 Great Britain, whose commercial interests in Japan were larger than those of any other Western nation, agreed to a revision of her treaty so that judicial rights would be restored to the Japanese in 1899. At the same time, partial tariff autonomy was recovered, complete autonomy following several years later. With

[10] Tariff autonomy involves the right of a nation to prescribe its own customs duties. The exercise of this right might, of course, be limited by voluntary treaties of reciprocity with other states.

the principal obstacle, Great Britain, out of the way, new treaties were promptly negotiated with the other powers.

In Japan, as in Europe, imperialism was an important corollary of nationalism. Japanese expansion, which has become a determining factor in Far Eastern politics, manifested itself in an attempt to absorb near-by islands and other territories. But the road to empire was a difficult one. In the north there stood Russia to dispute the reassertion of Japanese sovereignty over the islands of Sakhalin, Yezo, and the Kurile group, while China was established in the southern islands and in Korea. Over the northern islands the Japanese government had traditionally exercised a shadowy control, but unfortunately they lay in the direct path of Russian expansion. In 1875 Japan was obliged to recognize Russia's title to Sakhalin in return for undisputed possession of the Kurile group. The acquisitive eyes of Japanese leaders were also cast toward the islands to the south of the main archipelago, the Riu Kiu (Liu Kiu) islands and Formosa. Here the imperialism of Japan met with a greater measure of success, chiefly because China, rather than Russia, was the obstacle. The Riu Kiu islands were claimed by both China and Japan, but the latter was prepared to weld them into her political system, while China could exert only the most nebulous control. After an attempted compromise had failed, Japan proceeded to hold the islands, turning a deaf ear to the protests which echoed from Peking. In Formosa the result was somewhat less decisive. As was so frequently the case in the international relations of China, the root of the difficulty lay in China's assertion of sovereignty plus her refusal of responsibility. A dispute over the treatment of shipwrecked Japanese sailors left Chinese sovereignty unimpaired but marked the island as a promising field for future Japanese expansion.

The Korean question was perhaps the most crucial of all. The Hermit Kingdom had long occupied an anomalous position in the policy of the Far East. With a magnificent lack of discrimination, she had sent present-bearing embassies not only to China, her overlord, but to Japan as well. Suspicious of Japan's new enthusiasm for Western ways, the Korean court refused to enter into further relations with the renegade and between 1867 and 1871 declined to receive three different missions from Tokyo. Meanwhile, in the peninsula, matters were going from bad to worse. Two parties were contending for supremacy, the conservatives who looked to China and the progressives whose inspiration was drawn from Japan. Twice the Japanese legation was subjected to indignities when a Chinese expedition attempted to put down revolts. Tokyo, therefore, took pains to prevent the recurrence of such episodes by obtaining the right to maintain troops in Seoul, the capital of Korea. As a further spur toward a vigorous Korean policy there was the menacing figure of Russia pressing south in search of an ice-free port. Should the chaotic peninsula fall into the hands of a strong power, Japanese security would be plainly threatened. At this stage in her internal reorganization, however, Japan was willing to risk war with neither Russia nor China. The net result was a joint agreement (1885) with China which pledged that neither side would send troops into Korea without giving "notice in writing of its intention to do so."

The significance of this imperialistic development in Japanese foreign policy is two-fold. In the first place, the way was being prepared for a struggle between the two leading Oriental states, China and Japan. The sources of conflict were clearly apparent in Formosa, in Korea, and in the Riu Kiu islands. Secondly, a collision between Japan and Russia moved within the realm of probability. Japanese statesmen were acutely aware of the necessity for drawing their sinews of war as well as raw material for their growing industries from the continent. To guarantee these it was necessary to prevent the aggression of a strong European power. It was equally important to demonstrate to the West that the new Japan was a force to be reckoned with, indeed, that it was fitted to act as the leader of the Far East.

THE SINO-JAPANESE WAR

A clash between the revivified Japan and China, still unshaken in her age-old conservatism, lay in the logic of history. Their interests, as we have pointed out, conflicted in Formosa, the Riu Kiu islands, and most of all, in Korea. Indeed, it was almost inevitable that there should be a war for dominance in the Hermit Kingdom. In 1894 another rebellion broke out in Seoul, and, when first China and then Japan despatched troops, the scene was laid for war.[11] Japan was so well prepared with her modernized army and fleet that the

[11] The Chinese sent word to Tokyo after troops had already been despatched, thus infringing the agreement of 1885.

issue was never in doubt. The forces of the islanders were everywhere successful, with victories to their credit in Korea, Manchuria, and the Liaotung peninsula. The treaty of Shimonoseki (1895), by which hostilities were brought to an end, marked an utter humiliation for China. She was obliged to recognize the complete independence of Korea; to cede to Japan Formosa, the Pescadores islands, and the Liaotung peninsula including Port Arthur; and to pay a large indemnity.

The Chinese were thoroughly appalled by their crushing defeat at the hands of a people whom they had traditionally regarded as semi-civilized barbarians, and whose sensational departure from Oriental paths they had regarded with hostility and contempt. Now, however, many of the Chinese themselves became interested in the civilization which had imparted such aggressive force to Japan, and numbers of them saw the need for reform in their own country. Eager as some few were, the time was not yet at hand when change should be the accepted program of official China. Further disgrace was still in store.

EUROPEAN IMPERIALISM IN CHINA

The powers of Europe were only slightly less surprised than China at the outcome of the war, for it had revealed a weakness in the Chinese state more serious than even they had suspected. Nor did they altogether relish the success which the parvenu Japan had achieved, with her possession of one of the most strategic positions on the entire continent, Port Arthur. The policy of European powers in 1895 was vastly different from what it had been in 1842 and 1858. Then, as we have already indicated, their course was dictated by their desire for commercial concessions, which all of the countries shared with each other. During the latter half of the century, however, their policies had changed to one of unashamed colonial expansion. The recrudescence of competitive nationalism had turned men's minds to overseas dominions, a greater France or Germany, which would provide an outlet for surplus population and capital, a source of raw materials, and a market, as well as satisfy the ambitions of the chauvinists. The days of the alliances and the race of armaments saw each country aspiring to make of itself an economic unit, to develop what may be termed a new mercantilism. Loans to finance railroads and mines or to reorganize feeble governments became the handmaid of political imperialism. It was literally "conquest by railroad and bank."

Thus to a group of nations governed by imperialist prepossessions the crying weakness of China was disclosed. In previous decades they had succeeded in lopping off the principal outlying dependencies such as Annam, Cochin China, and Burma. Now the collapse of the whole structure seemed imminent. No power was more interested than Russia in the outcome of events. The diplomatic defeat which Russia had suffered at the Congress of Berlin (1878) had diverted her attention from the Balkans to the Middle and Far East as fields for expansion. She had undertaken the construction of the trans-Siberian railway, the chain which would bind together her scattered dominions. Unfortunately, her Pacific port, Vladivostok, was navigable only during the summer months, and she was eager for a harbor in the south which would be ice-free twelve months in the year. Her concern became consternation when, by the treaty of Shimonoseki, Japan acquired the Liaotung peninsula, which Russia regarded as the logical site for her future ports. In opposing Japanese expansion, Russia was joined by Germany and France. The three powers protested and forced Japan to re-cede the peninsula to China in return for a larger indemnity.[12] As a price for her good offices to China, Russia was permitted to lay her railway across northern Manchuria. It was also a part of the Russian design that the Liaotung peninsula ultimately should become the domain of the Tsar, in fact, if not in name.

THE LEASED PORTS

In 1897 two German missionaries in Shantung were murdered, and the German government, invoking a principle by no means new in the dealings of Europe with China, demanded as compensation valuable mining and railway concessions in Shantung and a ninety-nine year lease of the shores of the bay of Kiaochow. The other powers now professed themselves alarmed over the destruction of the balance of power in the Far East and eager to redress it. Russia and France now

[12] "It is not yet possible to trace the origin of the three-power intervention. The best available evidence points to Russia, but there are some who hold either France or Germany responsible. . . . France, the ally of Russia, might be expected to support her desires, especially when it offered a chance to win favor in China. And Germany probably was influenced both by a willingness to win the good will of Russia, her powerful neighbor, and the desire to play an influential part in the politics of the Far East." Treat, *The Far East*, pp. 304-305.

pushed their demands to the front, for China already owed them a debt of gratitude for their intervention after Shimonoseki, a debt which they intended to collect in full. The Russians contented themselves with the southern tip of Liaotung peninsula, including Port Arthur and Dalny, and with permission to connect these new possessions with the trans-Siberian by means of a railway through southern Manchuria. France obtained a lease of the bay of Kwangchow in southern China, the section where her interests were predominant.

This welter of aggression placed Great Britain in a difficult position. With all her previous assaults upon Chinese exclusiveness, she had never sought to acquire territory.[13] In fact, the policy of the British had been to open China to trade but to preserve the territorial integrity of the decadent empire. Even in 1898 Great Britain had no great desire to depart from her tradition by demanding Chinese land. But it could hardly have been expected that she would stand complaisantly aside while her diplomatic rivals were carving China up in accordance with their national ambitions. The British therefore demanded and received the port of Weihaiwei on the northern shore of the Shantung peninsula. This lease was obviously intended as a counterpoise to the threatening advance of Russia, at the time, her great diplomatic enemy. Weihaiwei was to

[13] The British acquisition of Burma can scarcely be regarded as an exception to this general statement, for Burma was bound to China only by the most shadowy of ties. Furthermore, the British had acted chiefly to forestall annexation by France. The cession of Hongkong, after the first Anglo-Chinese war, was demanded because of the need for a trading base.

be held "for so long a period as Port Arthur shall remain in the occupation of Russia."

THE "BATTLE OF CONCESSIONS"

The leasing of territory by no means ended the humiliation of China at the hands of the powers. The demands of the Russians and Germans, including as they did important railway concessions, virtually created spheres of influence for these two powers in Manchuria and Shantung. As early as 1895, when her protest had helped to revise the treaty of Shimonoseki, France had marked the three southern provinces of the empire as her economic preserve, while in the Yangtse valley British interests were paramount. The term "sphere of influence" is a rather vague one. Usually the nation holding the sphere is given a monopoly of railway and, perhaps, mining concessions, or at least a preferential right to supply capital for such enterprises. After the powers had staked out their claims, either actually or by implication, there ensued a series of frenetic struggles between rival groups of capitalists, supported by their respective foreign offices, for the privilege of financing the railways which the Chinese government had reluctantly decided to build. Each power sought to capture for itself as many of the prizes of economic imperialism as possible, and at the same time to protect its sphere from economic penetration by the financiers of another nation. Thus when a railway projected by Franco-Russian interests threatened to impair the hold of the British on the Yangtse valley, the matter was made the subject of frantic representations to Peking. The British government professed to regard the granting of this concession as an "act of deliberate hostility." Ultimately the powers were obliged to enter into agreements with each other which restricted their concessions to their own spheres of influence.

The delimitation of European spheres of influence implied much more than a group of railway-building monopolies. At the time it seemed highly probable that the ancient empire would succumb to the onslaught of Western imperialism and would suffer complete dismemberment. In marking out their spheres the powers were also registering their claims for territory, to be enforced whenever the partition of China occurred. Thus both the Anglo-Chinese and the Franco-Chinese agreements of 1898 prohibited China from ceding or leasing territory in either sphere to a third power. It may be safely inferred that Russia and Germany held similar designs. In short, the self-appointed legatees of the Chinese empire had already arranged for the division of the estate.

THE OPEN DOOR DOCTRINE

In the years immediately following the Sino-Japanese war, then, dismemberment seemed a probable destiny for the ancient empire. Indeed, China owed her escape not to any genuine eagerness for reform. The Chinese people were only slowly awakening to the need for change. By their contact with the West, possibly a few thousands of the educated classes had perceived that the country must be modernized, but these thousands were impotent before the ponderous inertia of their millions of countrymen. The war with Japan and the subsequent humiliation at the hands of the powers, to be sure, had provided a graphic object lesson for the more intelligent of the masses, even though they possessed little understanding of the intricacies of diplomacy. Nevertheless, China was saved from partition not so much by the growth of reformism as by two more or less fortuitous events: the proclamation of the open door policy, by which the powers pledged themselves to respect treaty rights within their spheres of influence; and secondly, the Boxer revolt, the last despairing gasp of the Old China, which demonstrated at once to the West the danger of goading China into desperate resistance and to the Chinese the bankruptcy of their old resources of anti-foreignism and exclusivism.

The United States had carefully abstained from participating in the battle for leased ports and spheres of influence. Indeed, during most of the nineteenth century, the American government had been utterly lacking in enthusiasm for overseas possessions. The Western world had provided ample field for expansion. By the close of the century, however, the frontier had disappeared, and after the war with Spain a rising spirit of imperialism inspired the annexation of the Philippines, the Hawaiian group, and certain smaller islands in the South Pacific. Furthermore, American commercial interests in China were of such significance that the Washington government viewed with alarm any attempt to restrict the economic opportunities of its citizens. Consequently, when the scramble for leased ports and spheres of influence threatened to carve China into the economic preserves of European nations, the apprehensions of the State Department were aroused.

The disapproval of the British was quite as pronounced as that of the Americans, although they were obliged to sacrifice their traditional policy and to demand a leased port and a sphere of influence. Nevertheless, their great interests in China were commercial, interests which might well be jeopardized by economic partition. The British government, therefore, suggested to Secretary of State John Hay that the two powers jointly declare against the violation of the open door in China. At the time the proposal was declined, but by September, 1899, the United States, partly as a result of other British influences, was ready to act independently.[14] Essentially, the open door policy, as enunciated in 1899, required that no power holding a leased port or sphere of influence should interfere with the vested interests of any other power nor should it give to its own nationals the benefit of preferential tariff or railroad rates. In short, the United States demanded that, regardless of the political control of Chinese territory, all foreigners should receive the commercial treatment to which they were entitled by their treaties with the Chinese government.

Secretary Hay addressed notes to the powers, requesting assurance that they intended to adhere to these principles. Assent was forthcoming from all of the countries consulted, Great Britain, Germany, Russia,

[14] For an account of British influence behind the open door notes, see A. L. P. Dennis, *Adventures in American Diplomacy*, Chapter VIII.

France, Japan, and Italy. It is important to observe that there was nothing novel about the doctrine as it was proclaimed in 1899, except for the term "open door." In fact, the principle had been at the heart of both British and American policy in China since the days of the Opium war. Its basis lay in the "most favored nation" clauses of the treaties, which virtually guaranteed equal treatment to citizens of treaty powers. Nevertheless, Hay's insistence on the open door was exceedingly opportune, coming at a time when the powers, to say the least, were complacent toward the utter disruption of the Chinese empire.

THE ABORTIVE REFORM MOVEMENT

Another factor which helped to stem the tide of Western aggression was the disastrous Boxer outbreak of 1900. Although the Boxers for the time being brought only further humiliation upon their country, yet ultimately their unfortunate exploits lent further strength to the hands of the reformers. We have already indicated that the war with Japan had impressed upon many thoughtful Chinese the necessity for fighting the West with its own weapons, and subsequent treatment by the powers confirmed their views and served to convince some, at least, of their less informed countrymen.

The center of the reform agitation was Canton, which had been longer in contact with foreigners than had other sections. Under the leadership of K'ang Yu-wei, a constitutional monarchist, there was aroused a sentiment in favor of westernization. From Canton it infected other provinces, until even Peking was touched by reform propaganda. The reformers won the support of the young emperor, who for a brief period emerged as the champion of change. A series of decrees was promulgated (1898), calling for a thoroughgoing reform of the empire. Many phases of Chinese life were comprehended by this veritable deluge of edicts which fell like rain upon the unsuspecting citizens. The army, education, especially technical education, railways, mines, judicial reform, permission to memorialise the emperor—these were some of the subjects dealt with by more than forty decrees issued within the brief space of three months. Everything was to be recast in the Western mold.

Unhappily for the reformers, the venerable empress dowager, though she had officially retired as regent, still continued to exercise enormous influence, and she was by no means unaware of the tremendous changes that had been legislated into effect. She correctly divined what neither the reformers nor the "mentally anemic" young emperor had sensed, that Europeanization was proceeding at a pace too rapid to be permanent. The advocates of change had been able to carry only a small minority of the country with them. Suddenly the empress struck. Having obtained the support of the army, she promptly interned the young emperor in the winter palace, seized the reins of power, and executed all the reformers she could lay her hands upon. Reaction was again in the saddle.

THE BOXERS

The spirit which was manifested in the *coup d'état* of the empress dowager revealed itself among the common people in the society of the Boxers, or "Fists of Public Harmony." The traditional account of the genesis of this sanguinary movement has recently undergone revision.[15] Formerly it was thought that the Boxers were merely one of the many revolutionary secret societies which have flourished throughout the history of China. It now appears, however, that they were originally bodies of local militia which were organized by the empress dowager after her seizure of power, chiefly to withstand foreign aggression. The same forces which had produced the reaction at court supported it in the provinces. The government, backed by an infuriated people, determined to resist further humiliation. Unfortunately, the Boxers, drawing to themselves the disorderly elements in the population, became increasingly violent in their anti-foreignism. At the same time, the foreign diplomats in Peking persisted in misinterpreting the movement. Apparently, they could not conceive of China as other than helpless and inert, and they failed utterly to see the uprising in its proper light, as a nationalist protest against the attacks of the West. By their demands upon the central government they lowered its prestige in the eyes of the country and eventually drove the Boxer movement beyond control.

In the anti-foreign outbreaks throughout North China, missionaries and their converts were the chief sufferers. The climax of the demonstration occurred at Peking, where the foreigners, who had gathered in the legation quarters, were besieged for two months, to be rescued finally by a joint force composed of

[15] G. N. Steiger, *China and the Occident.*

British, Japanese, Russian, French, Germans, and Americans. The vandalism displayed by the allied troops in sacking the city, particularly the magnificent imperial palace, rivalled the ignorant brutality of the Boxers themselves.

China was made to pay dearly for her temerity, not only in money and concessions but in that somewhat undefinable "loss of face" so dear to the heart of the old-school Chinese. The government was forced to send missions of apology to the West and to execute the principal official instigators of the uprising. A huge indemnity was imposed, admittedly out of all proportion to the legitimate claims of foreigners. The Manchu régime was obliged to allow foreign garrisons in Peking and along the route to the sea.

THE FAR EAST AT THE TURN OF THE CENTURY

China had now sounded the depths of national degradation. She had received a crushing defeat from the Japanese, whom she had considered inferior barbarians. She had been assaulted by the economic and, in some degree, the political imperialism of the West. The popular movement to evict the foreigner and all his works had been ruthlessly suppressed and from it all China had apparently reaped nothing but further disgrace. Yet the outlook was not altogether hopeless. If, on the one hand, the Boxer outbreak had disclosed a deep-seated resentment against European nations and had demonstrated to the world that even the Chinese worm might turn, on the other, it had shown even the most obtuse and unregenerate leader that some measure of reform was inevitable.

Across the sea of Japan a vastly different situation prevailed. If Commodore Perry had been able to visit the islands at the end of the century he might well have concluded that he had landed upon another planet. The changes that would have met his eyes he would have found quite unbelievable. Within the space of fifty years, an Oriental state had completely transformed its political and economic system. The world has rarely seen such an astounding transition accomplished with so few missteps.[16] To be sure, mistakes were made. As one historian has observed, "There was a certain element of incongruity and even grotesqueness in the nation's doings. Old people cannot fit their feet to new roads without some clumsiness. The Japanese had grown very old in their special paths, and their novel departure was occasionally disfigured by solecisms." It is probably true to say that westernization has been applied chiefly to externals,

[16] The comparatively smooth transition which Japan effected stands in striking contrast to the chaos which has been China's experience as she has attempted to adjust her life to the new conditions. No explanation is altogether satisfactory, although some possible reasons may be hinted at. In the first place, it may be observed that the task of the Chinese was infinitely more difficult. An index of this difference may be obtained by comparing the areas and populations of the two countries. Furthermore, the background of the Japanese prepared them for the new forms. For example, the shogunate, at least during certain stages in its existence, enforced a rather high degree of centralization. The discipline and loyalty of the military class were qualities no less valuable to the New Japan than to the Old. The tradition of continuity which the emperor provided, formed a rallying point for all the forces of nationalism. Finally, it should be repeated that assimilation of foreign civilizations was a part of the Japanese past. "Japan had for centuries been accustomed to embrace and adapt new ideas from abroad. . . . In this again she had the advantage of China. That country had never known intimately a culture equal to her own. It had for centuries posed as a teacher, not a learner." Latourette, *Development of Japan,* p. 90.

and that the private life of the Japanese is still surprisingly Oriental. Nevertheless, the dominant impression left on the student is not that of a savage chieftain who suddenly determines to assume European dress and who cuts, to say the least, a fantastic figure, but of a people whose fine sense of discrimination enables them to select the best from the new without sacrificing the treasured heritage from the old.

CHAPTER III

CHINA AND JAPAN IN WORLD POLITICS,
1901-1928

DURING the last quarter-century, especially during the last decade, the eyes of the world have been increasingly focussed upon the Far East. Diplomatists and business men, naval chiefs and missionary boards have found insistent problems in the unparalleled state of affairs in the Orient. Mere observers are fascinated by the drama of the changing East, where the charm of the older civilization mingles incongruously with the utilitarianism of the newer, where the sixteenth century rubs casual elbows with the twentieth. The future of this Orient is both an alluring field for the genius with the gift of prophecy and a world problem of transcendent importance.

Since the turn of the century, the evolution of the Far East has been determined, in a large degree, by three factors. First of all, there is the ascent of Japan into the ranks of the great powers. As we have seen, Japan had already received formal recognition as a sovereign state and had demonstrated her military superiority over China. But she had yet to establish her right to a place among the great European states. This she accomplished dramatically enough, when she concluded a diplomatic alliance with Great Britain and then proceeded to inflict a decisive defeat upon Russia. A second element is the renaissance of China, perhaps the most extraordinary pageant of its kind the world has ever witnessed. Before our sight one-fifth of the people of the globe are moving from the middle ages into the modern day, attempting to realign their traditional mode of life with the demands of the twentieth century, and, at the same time, to gain for their country a place of dignity and respect in the family of nations. Finally, one must observe the policies pursued by European nations and Japan in regard to Chinese questions. Since the Great War the Far East has been indubitably one of the danger spots in international relations, holding rich possibilities of war both between China and the powers and between Western nations themselves. To-day, the interaction of these two forces, a revolutionary China and a West, uncertain and groping in its policies, offers a fascinating field for study, the more so because the outcome is not to be foreseen.

THE ANGLO-JAPANESE ALLIANCE

In the years immediately following the Boxer crisis, the most troublesome diplomatic question in the Far East was created by the policy of Russia. The government at St. Petersburg saw in the unsettled conditions an opportunity to achieve its long-treasured imperialistic ambitions. We have already remarked Russia's political and economic penetration of Manchuria. During the confusion of the Boxer year, she had been strengthening her hold on that area, pouring in troops which she made no effort to withdraw when the danger had passed. Moreover, she was threatening to absorb Korea itself.

For this latter region to fall under Russian control meant a barrier to the expansion of Japan and a powerful enemy at her very gate. The most promising field for Japanese economic penetration and emigration would thus be closed. The Japanese felt that their only hope of security was to block Russia before she could possess Korea, whose weak, corrupt government could offer no effective resistance. Nor were the Japanese unmindful of Russian intervention in 1895, which had deprived them of the fruits of their victory over China.

At one with Japan in her fear of Russia was Great Britain. The Slav had already made menacing gestures at the northwestern frontier of India, and his agents in Persia and Afghanistan were a perennial source of apprehension to British statesmen. The obvious intention of the Tsar's government to violate the open door in Manchuria and to become the paramount power in north China provided still further cause for alarm. On the basis of their mutual fear of Russian advance in the Far East, therefore, the two powers in 1902 negotiated the Anglo-Japanese alliance. The treaty was a rather curious document in that it guaranteed Japan a great deal and Great Britain very little. If either party were attacked by a third power in such a way that its vital interests in the Far East were threatened, the other would remain neutral and would use its influence to preserve the neutrality of other powers. In case another nation came to the aid of the aggressor, Great Britain and Japan were to wage war together.

The striking feature of the first treaty of alliance is that it related only to the interests of the two powers in China and Korea, thus leaving England to handle her Indian frontier alone. The explanation of the favorable bargain which Japan received lies chiefly in the diplomatic isolation of Great Britain and the growing anxiety of British statesmen in regard to it. The Triple Alliance comprised Austria, Germany, and Italy; the Dual Alliance, France and Russia, but Great Britain still preserved what she had been pleased to term "splendid isolation"—seclusion that was daily appearing less splendid in a period of diplomatic tension. In 1905, when the Anglo-Japanese alliance was renewed, it was extended to include India. Great Britain also agreed to recognize the paramount interests of Japan in Korea.

THE RUSSO-JAPANESE WAR

Even though reënforced by her alliance with Great Britain, Japan was eager to bring her difficulties with Russia to peaceable settlement. The Japanese regarded Korea as their field of special interest, and they were willing that, as compensation, Russia should do as she pleased in Manchuria, providing that the open door and the territorial integrity of China were respected. That is, Russia might have Manchuria, if she would relinquish her designs upon Korea. The Japanese sought to reach an understanding with their rivals, but a protracted series of negotiations produced only further delay.[1]   No alternative seemed open to Tokyo but an appeal to arms.   Diplomatic relations were broken off on February 6, 1904, and war was declared four days later.

Once convinced that open hostilities were inevitable, the Japanese struck like lightning and waged the war flawlessly.   The fighting centered around Port Arthur and Mukden, the capital of Manchuria.   After a tedious siege, General Nogi captured Port Arthur in January, 1905, and when, a few weeks later, the Russians were defeated at Mukden, the military objectives of the Japanese had been largely realized.   On the sea the Russians fared no less badly.   Their Baltic fleet, part of which had reached Eastern waters by way of the Cape of Good Hope, was completely shattered by Admiral Togo.   Throughout the war the Russians were hopelessly outgeneraled.   The individual heroism of the Russian troops counted for little beside the corrupt, inefficient administration and dissension in St. Petersburg.

With her military forces everywhere victorious, Japan was now in an admirable position from which to negotiate a satisfactory peace.   At the suggestion of Japan, President Roosevelt offered to mediate.   The Japanese, of course, accepted at once, while the Russians, embarrassed by a revolution at home, were al-

[1] The least unsatisfactory proposals that could be obtained from St. Petersburg would have "allowed Russia a free hand in China and Manchuria, while Russia was to allow Japan to develop only industrial and commercial interests in Korea, a development which Russia had previously shown herself powerless to prevent." Vinacke, *History of the Far East*, pp. 167-68.   After much delay, the Russians offered other concessions, but the dispatch did not arrive in Tokyo until after diplomatic relations had been severed.

most obliged to enter into negotiations. By the treaty
of Portsmouth (September, 1905) Japan recovered all
that she had lost through the intervention of Russia,
France, and Germany after Shimonoseki, as well as
making other substantial gains. She made good her
claim to Korea, first administering it as a protector-
ate and, five years later, annexing it outright. Russia's
railways and mining concessions in southern Manchuria were transferred to her, together with the lease
of Port Arthur. Both powers agreed to evacuate
Manchuria and to recognize the sovereignty of China.
Japan also received the southern half of the island of
Sakhalin, which Russia had acquired at her expense
in 1875.

Japan had more than vindicated her position as a
world power. Within an incredibly short space of
time she had been transformed from a secluded feudal
state into a modern nation that had defeated one of
the most powerful military organizations of the West.
She had achieved recognition in an alliance with Great
Britain. By her victory over Russia she saw her imperialistic policy crowned with success and the future
respect of the West assured.

REFORM IN CHINA

The defeat of the hitherto invincible Westerner at
the hands of an Asiatic nation affected the Chinese profoundly. To the painful evidence already impressed
upon them by the Sino-Japanese war, the "battle
of concessions," and the Boxer year was added that
of the late war. The Chinese were further humiliated
by the fact that most of the fighting had taken place

upon Chinese soil, a violation of sovereignty which Peking was impotent to prevent. Yet the practical demonstration of what could be done by an Oriental state that had assimilated the material civilization of the West was an inspiration to the discouraged Chinese. The weight of the argument, therefore, was plainly on the side of westernization.

At last conservative China bowed to the inevitable, and the program of reform, timidly begun in 1900, was infused with new vigor. The once exclusive Middle Kingdom now became most cordial to foreigners, who were encouraged to live in the country and to give their tutelage to the groping Chinese. For better or for worse, the two peoples must live together. Even the empress dowager displayed an apparent change of heart. On her return to Peking after the Boxer crisis, she did everything to impress her hospitality upon foreign residents, even going to the unheard-of extreme of receiving the ladies of the embassies at court and showering them with presents and apologies. Thousands of Chinese were enrolled in the universities of Japan and the West. In 1906 there were 13,000 in Japan alone. Elaborate plans were laid for the creation of a new educational system. A step of the utmost significance was taken in 1905 when a single decree swept away the old system of examinations and substituted one composed, in a large measure, of Western subjects. Parallel with the destruction of the old went the creation of the new. By the end of 1909 there were more than 57,000 government schools, including five "universities."

The work of railroad construction which had been

almost in abeyance since 1895 again occupied the center of the stage. By 1910 there were more than 3000 miles in operation and 1550 under construction. The new found nationalism of the Chinese manifested itself in a movement for regaining control over lines for which concessions had been granted to foreigners. When, for example, arrangements were made for the construction of three new roads, great care was taken that management should be left in Chinese hands. An impetus was also given to improved communications of other kinds. By 1906 there were more than 3000 miles of telegraph lines, while the postal service established in 1906 grew so rapidly that by 1910 there were some 4000 offices. China was proceeding eagerly, even feverishly, along the road to Europeanization. Whereas, after the Boxer uprising, it had been only the Manchus and other leaders who perceived the necessity for some degree of change, now even the illiterate classes, inspired by the amazing success of Japan, revealed a new spirit of nationalism in their enthusiasm for reform.

POLITICAL CHANGES

Simultaneously with these sweeping economic and social changes there was proceeding a gradual reorganization of the government. In 1906 an imperial edict projected the reform of the army and navy, the law courts, the finances, and the administrative system of the empire. Meanwhile, the demand for constitutional government, emanating chiefly from students who had absorbed liberal ideas abroad, became so insistent that no longer could it be complacently ignored.

In 1905 a commission was appointed to study the governmental systems of foreign countries, with a view to their adaptation for use in China. After full weight had been given to the commission's report, a decree was issued promising representative government. To prepare the way for this millennium, the empress dowager proposed that provincial assemblies, vested with advisory powers only, should be convoked in 1909, followed by a national assembly in 1910, and a genuine parliament in 1915. Whether such measures were honestly intended to educate the people for constitutional government or were merely a sop to the reformers will never be known. Before the program was well under way, the empress died, leaving the throne to a baby emperor and a regent, who was amiable enough but quite inexperienced. With the passing of this remarkable woman the Manchus lost their last able leader, and the collapse of the dynasty became only a matter of time.

THE CHINESE REVOLUTION

The weakening of the central government at this crisis played into the hands of the radicals, who felt that the progress toward constitutionalism was altogether too deliberate. When the provincial assemblies met for the first time, they demanded that parliament should meet two years earlier than had been originally planned. The intransigent attitude assumed by the Manchus who were still in control at Peking lent strength to the democratic movement, long agitated in South China, and it naturally expressed itself in plots and revolutionary activities against the alien dynasty, symbolic of foreign domination. The indefatigable Sun Yat-sen, democrat and nationalist, had traveled among the Chinese in the Occident, often at great personal risk, preaching republican doctrines, and many revolutionary societies had been formed among the people, particularly in the progressive South.

The dénouement, however, came with dramatic precipitancy, surprising even most of the radicals themselves. The occasion was merely the arrest of a band of revolutionaries at Hankow, in central China. Against this the radicals protested forcibly, supported by mutinous imperial troops. Beginning in west and central China, where the railway policy of the Peking government had produced a state of unrest, the flame of revolt swept down the valley of the Yangtse.[2] By December, 1911, most of the southern provinces had declared their independence. The Manchu regent recalled General Yüan Shih-k'ai, who had been in disgrace, to take command of the imperial army. Aware of the power of the revolutionary movement the prudent Yüan strongly advised that the dynasty abdicate. His counsel was accepted, and the Manchu house agreed to "retire into leisure to pass easily through the months and years and to see the consummation of wise government," as the edict of abdication euphemistically put it. Meanwhile, the provinces of the South had organized themselves into a republic with Sun Yat-sen as president. The climax of the revolutionary

[2] The central government proposed to absorb and complete certain railway lines which had been begun under provincial auspices. A foreign loan was to be used to finance the undertaking. This project resulted in widespread popular demonstrations, which the revolutionaries astutely used for their own ends.

movement came with the formation of a united Chinese republic (1912) under the presidency of Yüan Shih-k'ai, in whose favor Dr. Sun gracefully stepped aside.

Although, as most students believe, the change to a republic was premature, yet it was probably inevitable. The pulsating national spirit found the rule of the alien and moribund Manchu dynasty intolerable, and no line of native rulers was available as a substitute. Furthermore, the years of civil war which have traditionally characterized changes of dynasties in China would have been quite suicidal in 1911-12. Under the circumstances a conservative republic appears to have been the best and, indeed, the only possible solution.[3]

Yüan Shih-k'ai, the new president, never believed wholeheartedly in the republic. Nor was it his intention to become a merely ornamental figure who would shine in the reflected glory of the assembly. The Southerners, on the other hand, with their intense democratic convictions, were in control of the assembly, where they proceeded to obstruct measures proposed by the president. Yüan, a political realist, saw clearly that these inexperienced and doctrinaire parliamentarians were obstacles in the path of reconstruction. Disgusted by their tactics and persuaded of the impracticability of the republic, he began to arrogate to himself more and more power. He expelled the radical party (Kuomintang) from the national assembly, dismissed the provincial bodies, and became virtually a military dictator. He inspired a demand that he assume the imperial throne, and, by

[3] See Latourette, *The Development of China,* pp. 209-10.

means of unblushing chicanery, he brought about his own election. Revolution again broke out in the South, and division seemed unavoidable, when, in the words of a Chinese writer, "Providence found a solution by calling Yüan Shih-k'ai to Heaven."

THE WORLD WAR IN THE FAR EAST

The internal situation in China, unpromising enough at best, was further complicated by the chaos of the World War. Although neither Japan nor China had a direct stake in the immediate issues of the conflict, they were drawn irresistibly into the vortex by their national interests. Great Britain and Japan, it will be recalled, had been bound together in an alliance since 1902, which had been renewed in 1905 and 1911. British fear of Russia in China had been allayed by the Russo-Japanese war, so that in 1907 the two were able to patch up their remaining difficulties and to cement the Triple Entente. Finally, the world saw the curious picture of a growing *rapprochement* between the late enemies, Japan and Russia. As a result of their war, Russia had given way to Japan in southern Manchuria but still retained her paramount position in the north. In 1907 and again in 1910 and 1912, they had consecrated this division of Manchuria into economic spheres and had contracted to preserve the *status quo*. In short, Japan had intimately associated herself with the Triple Entente.

The Japanese, though not legally bound to enter the struggle unless Britain were attacked in India or the Far East, were by no means reluctant to interpret the alliance broadly. In reality, however, the alliance had very little to do with Japan's determination to make war. It was chiefly Japanese ambitions on the mainland of Asia that brought her into the conflict, and it was there that her most significant wartime exploits took place. Statesmen in Tokyo had long realized the importance of controlling the rich market and the reservoir of raw materials on the continent. Here at last, with European nations at each other's throats, was an admirable opportunity to ensure the future position of Japan. She could now make good her claim to leadership in Far Eastern affairs; indeed, could dictate terms to her European allies as well as to China. Accordingly, on August 23, 1914, war was declared against Germany, and an attack upon Tsing-tao, the German leased port in Shantung, was begun immediately. In November, the city fell, whereupon the Japanese appropriated not merely the port itself, but the other rights and properties, such as railways and mines, which the Germans had held in Shantung.

THE TWENTY-ONE DEMANDS

In January, Japan adopted a course which made her attitude toward China quite unmistakable. First of all, she served upon Peking the notorious "twenty-one demands," which, in a word, would have made Japanese influence paramount in certain sections of China. Included in the demands were such extraordinary requisitions as the following: that China assent to any arrangement which Japan might make with Germany in regard to the latter's holdings in Shantung; that the largest mining and smelting company in China be made a joint Sino-Japanese enterprise; and that China contract not to lease territory along her coast to a third power. When the Chinese government showed a disposition to engage in diplomatic fencing, the Japanese minister presented an ultimatum requiring the immediate acceptance of four of the five groups of demands in revised form.[4] The especially odious fifth group, which would have given Japan complete control over her ponderous and confused neighbor, was reserved for future discussion because of the tremendous wave of protest that arose from China.[5] In this group were such demands as the following: that Japanese advisers must be employed in the Peking government; that fifty per cent or more of China's munitions of war must be purchased from Japanese; and that certain districts be policed jointly by the two countries. Fearful at once of military intervention and of incurring Japanese opposition to his private ambitions, Yüan Shih-k'ai accepted the first four groups with substantial modifications in China's favor. The fifth group provided Japan with an admirable weapon with which to wrest less obnoxious concessions. In the treaties of 1915, by which China formally accepted the four groups, Japanese economic hegemony was assured in southern Manchuria, eastern inner Mongolia, and Shantung.[6] Japan

[4] The demands, as originally presented, included five groups, dealing respectively with Shantung, southern Manchuria and eastern inner Mongolia, the iron works at Hanyang, non-alienation of territory along the coast, and a fifth group of miscellaneous demands.

[5] It is an open question whether the Japanese government expected the fifth group to be acted upon by the Chinese. They were to be regarded as "the wishes of the Imperial Government" and "entirely different in character from those which are included in the first four groups."

[6] Some of the demands were accepted in treaties, others in exchanges of notes, while one was settled by China's making a public declaration of policy. This was the article which prohibited China from leasing or ceding territory along her coast to a third power.

thus became the indubitable leader of the Far East, but her leadership was erected upon precarious foundations. She had forfeited the prestige which she had enjoyed with the Chinese immediately after the Russo-Japanese war, when they had hailed her as the defender of the East against an imperialistic West.

Having enthroned herself as sovereign of the Orient in fact, Japan was eager to have her new position recognized by other nations, especially by the United States. Accordingly, envoys were sent to Washington to negotiate an agreement, which would place the stamp of world recognition upon her leadership. The result was the Lansing-Ishii agreement (November, 1917). Violating the terms of the engagement, the Japanese legation in Peking gave out a Chinese translation of the text. The provisions were innocuous enough, but, in the translation, they appeared to the Chinese as a complete abdication of the historic American policy. The agreement merely conceded the obvious fact that "Japan has special interests in China, particularly in that part to which her possessions are contiguous." In the language of diplomacy this might mean very little or a great deal, and the Chinese preferred to interpret it in the latter sense.

CHINA IN THE WAR AND AT THE PEACE CONFERENCE

During the early years of the war China had maintained an attitude of strict neutrality. Her own house was too chaotic to permit her participation in neighborhood brawls. In fact, many influential Chinese had leaned toward the Central Powers, repelled from the Allies by the presence of Japan. When, however, the

United States espoused the cause of the Allies, sentiment in China quickly turned toward participation, inspired partly by the idealistic pronouncements of
President Wilson. A further argument was the wholly
practical one of gaining a seat at the peace conference
and of obtaining, thereby, a voice in the settlement of
the Shantung and other Far Eastern questions. Notwithstanding the fact that the issue precipitated a
serious internal crisis, war was declared in August,
1917. Aside from sending a large number of coolies to
France as laborers, China took no more than a passive
part in the hostilities, for conditions within the country
were bordering on anarchy, and the international question had been all but lost sight of in the conflict of
personal ambitions at Peking.

The war had so engrossed the attention of European
powers that Japan was able to realize her ambitions
in China unobstructed. The Chinese, however, hoped
that redress might be obtained at the peace conference.
Their representatives went to Paris with hopes raised
high by the war aims of President Wilson. At last,
they felt, the weaker nations were to enter upon their
millennial day. The Chinese delegation demanded,
justly one would say, that the holdings of Germany in
China which had been appropriated by Japan be restored to their original owner. But they were doomed
to utter disillusionment.

Unfortunately for the Chinese case the Shantung
question had been prejudged in the summer of 1917
by a series of secret conventions between Japan and
the European Allies. Because of the havoc worked
by the German submarine campaign in the Mediter-

ranean, it had been necessary to purchase Japan's whole-hearted naval support. By these engagements, all German properties and leased territories in Shantung and all of the German colonies north of the equator were to be transferred outright to Japan. The peace conference recognized the validity of these secret treaties, despite the resistance of President Wilson, who capitulated only when the Japanese delegation threatened to withdraw from the conference. The Japanese accepted the gift of Shantung with a vague assurance that ultimately the rights should revert to China. Indignant at the treatment they had received, the representatives of China refused to sign the German treaty but obtained membership in the League of Nations by becoming signatories to the treaty of St. Germain with Austria. In 1921 the Chinese negotiated a separate peace with Germany.

THE PROBLEM OF THE PACIFIC

The Paris conference, it may be inferred, had implicitly conceded to Japan the leadership in the Far East, in that it had recognized the validity of the secret agreements of 1917 and had made no serious attempt to deprive her of the spoils of her wartime diplomacy.[7] There could be no reasonable doubt about the paramount position of Japan. She held the islands that guarded the coast of Asia from Formosa to Sakhalin. On the mainland her politico-economic imperialism had given her control of the territory from Shan-

[7] It should be pointed out that Japan was given the mandates for German colonies north of the equator. She therefore held them under the League.

tung to southern Manchuria and eastern inner Mongolia, including Korea.

The Allies, however, had many misgivings about the hegemony of Japan in the Pacific. Particularly apprehensive were the Americans, who feared that the extension of Japanese influence would endanger the safety of their interests, both political and commercial. If American commerce were to prosper the open door must be preserved in China and no one nation allowed to dominate. Closely allied to the question of Japanese hegemony in the Orient was that of naval armaments. Obviously no limitation in armaments could take place unless some attempt were made to adjust the conflicts in policy which were most likely to necessitate the use of navies. Perhaps the most crucial issues were those which concerned the Pacific basin, where a fresh contest in naval armaments seemed about to occur. Such a race would certainly involve the United States and Japan, and the former power, at least, was eager that the Far Eastern question be made the subject of an international discussion. The Washington government, it seems but fair to concede, was influenced not alone by disinterested concern for the peace of the world but also by solicitude for the imperial and commercial position of the United States in the Orient, especially for the security of the Philippines. American interests, it was believed, would never be safe as long as Japan, reënforced by the Anglo-Japanese alliance, maintained her dominance. In her suspicion of the alliance, the United States was supported by many British leaders and by the dominions, Canada, New Zealand, and Australia, who held it to be an em-

barrassing liaison since the German menace was out
of the way.

THE WASHINGTON CONFERENCE

Moved by these considerations, the American government invited the principal allied powers to meet
in conference at Washington during the winter of
1921-22. The agenda included questions relating to
naval armaments and the Far East. The settlement
finally reached was an exceedingly complicated one,
but it is important to recall some of the provisions
which related to the Orient. In the first place, the
treaty which limited naval armaments also prohibited
new fortifications in most of the European possessions
in the Pacific. This was a concession to the Japanese
demand for security. Secondly, the *status quo* in the
Far East was recognized by a four-power treaty between France, Great Britain, Japan, and the United
States by which the signatories agreed to respect each
other's territorial possessions. By this agreement the
Anglo-Japanese alliance was automatically terminated.
Thirdly, the nine powers present at the conference
covenanted to respect the integrity of China, to give
her an opportunity to stabilize her affairs, to maintain
the open door, and "to refrain from taking advantage
of conditions in China in order to seek special rights
or privileges which would abridge the rights of subjects or citizens of friendly states."

Two other acts of the conference have proved to be
of great importance. In another nine-power treaty
the powers bound themselves to call a special tariff
conference and promised to raise the tariff in China

immediately to an effective five per cent *ad valorem*. This represented a partial concession to the demands of the Chinese, although the latter had hoped to obtain complete tariff autonomy. The conference also agreed to the appointment of a commission to inquire into extra-territoriality in China, with a view to removing "immediately or as soon as circumstances will permit existing limitations upon China's political, jurisdictional and administrative sovereignty."

The most irritating of all Far Eastern questions, that of Shantung, was settled at the conference but not in it. There were obvious reasons why the matter could not be discussed in an official session, especially when six of the nine powers present had signed the treaty of Versailles. Through the influence of Mr. Hughes and Mr. Balfour the Chinese and Japanese delegations consented to discuss the question *vis-à-vis*. The Japanese had apparently sensed the disapproval with which much of the Western world regarded their policies. They now brought the matter to a conclusion on terms which, if not precisely generous, were at least satisfactory to the Chinese. Japan was to restore to China the leased territory which she had captured from Germany and was to surrender the Shantung railway with compensation. This agreement removed the most active source of friction between the two countries, but it alone could scarcely be expected to inaugurate an era of good feeling. The memory of the "twenty-one demands" still rankled, especially when the Japanese refused to abrogate those which had been accepted. Furthermore, as they relinquished their hold upon

Shantung, they clung even more tenaciously to Manchuria.

CHINESE POLITICS SINCE 1915

Chinese politics during the last fifteen years afford material for a melancholy chronicle. The details are not only obscure and confusing to the Westerner, but, in general, they are of little importance in such a survey as this. Essentially, the period has been one of conflict between parties and leaders, most of them utterly devoid of program other than their personal ambitions. The stage has been occupied by rival military chiefs, avidly contending for power, each backed by his semi-private army. Not the least striking feature of the situation has been the absence of all central government. To the Chinese this condition is much less embarrassing than it would be to an Occidental people, for the former, as a recent writer has observed, "are perhaps more nearly capable of national existence without government than would be any other of the civilized nations." Nevertheless, both in respect to internal administration and in dealing with foreign powers, the lack of a generally recognized central government imposed a severe handicap upon the country. Between 1917 and the reuniting of the state under the nationalist party in the summer of 1928, there was no agency that could be dignified as the national government of China. It would be footless to review the details of sordid struggles between rival military chiefs and cliques which occupied the intervening period. Our emphasis, rather, will be placed upon the rise to power of the nationalist party, or Kuomintang, with whose future the destiny of China seems to be closely bound up.

THE EMERGENCE OF THE TUCHUNS

The death of Yüan Shih-K'ai in 1916 renewed the optimism of the parliamentarians, who had ascribed the failure of constitutional government to the ambitions of the president rather than to their own tactics and the political immaturity of the people. Unhappily the tension between the executive and the dominant party in the legislature was in nowise alleviated. The conflict continued unabated, until in 1917 the constitutionalists, representing the southern provinces, seceded and established their own régime at Canton. Meanwhile, in Peking, the government fell into the hands of a pro-Japanese clique supported by a parliament in turn controlled by the *tuchuns* or military governors.

The struggle which resulted in the secession of the southern constitutionalists thus left the northern military leaders in control of the state. From 1917 to 1927-28 these warlords dominated the political scene, although they were by no means able to agree among themselves. The importance of the military chief dates from the revolution of 1911. The revolution and the confused years that followed resulted in the creation of large forces of men under arms commanded by irresponsible military leaders. These might give their allegiance to the regular provincial governor or to a self-appointed chieftain. In either case, the man who received their support was, in fact, the governor of the district. Yüan Shih-k'ai had been forced to legalize this anomalous arrangement by giving the *tuchuns* a regular place in his governmental system.

It was the northern *tuchuns* who were in command of the situation after 1917. The Peking government merely represented one faction or another of these actual rulers. Meanwhile, they devoted themselves to consolidating their position in the provinces, raising and equipping troops, collecting and disbursing taxes on their own initiative, and eagerly looked forward to the day when Peking should be their personal property. After 1920, civil war was almost perpetual, now among individual military leaders, now among their shifting coalitions, then between the north and the south, at times subsiding into an armed truce, again blazing forth with fierce intensity. For more than a year, indeed, the Chinese state was without even a nominal head.

THE RISE OF THE NATIONALIST PARTY

The Kuomintang, or nationalist party, which in 1928 achieved dominance in Chinese politics, owes its origin to the activities of Dr. Sun Yat-sen prior to the revolution of 1911. In the first parliament it was this group which so bitterly opposed Yüan Shih-k'ai in his efforts to enthrone himself as emperor. Later, as we have seen, the Kuomintang parliamentarians seceded, and, after some vicissitudes, in 1921 they formed the Chinese republic at Canton with Sun Yat-sen as president. This government sought to unify the seven southern provinces, though at first, it must be admitted, with indifferent success. The nationalists hoped to develop strength sufficient to capture the government of the country and to evict the corrupt and inept administration in Peking.

Meanwhile, the party was drawing new and influential support to its program. Large numbers of patriotic students, outraged by the Shantung settlement, were attracted to the Kuomintang. An alliance of equal significance was that entered into with the Soviet government of Russia. Radical Chinese had observed the socialistic experiment with intense interest, and, in fact, a number of those who visited Russia returned as enthusiastic communists. The Bolshevists were no less interested in cultivating an *entente cordiale* with the largest state of the Far East. In the Kuomintang appeared an admirable vehicle for the gospel of communism, if the party could be turned into the agent of a real nationalistic-revolutionary movement. Soviet propaganda was therefore pushed with all vigor in the ranks of labor and students.[8] It was primarily the anti-imperialist attitude of Moscow rather than its economic program that appealed to Chinese nationalists. If the purpose of the Bolshevists were really, as they professed, "to prevent Japan from absorbing Manchuria and to enable China to fight foreign imperialism," there was ground for eloquent appeal to patriotic Chinese.

Around the Russian high adviser to the Kuomintang was created a corps of military experts to reorganize the army, while at the same time there was begun the

[8] The Bolsheviks paid assiduous court to the Peking government as well, and, in 1924, they negotiated a treaty by which they relinquished extra-territoriality, a privilege which China had already withdrawn arbitrarily.

reconstruction of the party after the Soviet pattern. The Kuomintang came to conceive of itself as a militant, responsible minority, much like the Russian communist party. Although the nationalists readily absorbed communist organization, it can hardly be said that the party as a whole espoused communist dogma. The official platform consisted of three principles developed by Dr. Sun Yat-sen. These were, first, the abolition of foreign control in China; secondly, popular government; thirdly, important social and economic reforms. With this creed, sloganized into "Nationalism, Democracy, and Socialism," the Kuomintang solicited the support of the country.

THE COMMUNIST HEGEMONY IN THE KUOMINTANG

Despite the fact that a majority neither of the Chinese leaders nor the rank and file of the Kuomintang regarded themselves as communists, nevertheless the power of that minority increased steadily during 1925 and 1926. After the death of Dr. Sun in the spring of 1925 there began a duel for leadership, which resulted in the eviction of the non-communists from the central executive committee. Under communist influence the work of organization went on rapidly. A brilliantly conducted campaign of propaganda disseminated the inspired prophecies of a national utopia for China. Western industrial technique, strikes and boycotts were used with devastating effect. Both factory and countryside were in protest against imperialistic control and against the domination of the military clique in Peking.

The nationalists had frequently debated the forcible

overthrow of the northern government. This, of course, would necessitate an army sufficiently powerful to encompass the military conquest of the country. By the summer of 1926 it was felt that the day for the nationalist march had arrived. Almost without opposition the armies of Chiang K'ai-shek, the young military leader of the Kuomintang, swept northward as far as the Yangtse. Hankow, the "Chicago of China," was taken, whereupon the nationalist capital was transferred to that city from Canton. Their momentum scarcely checked, the victorious forces of Chiang K'ai-shek moved eastward, and by the spring of 1927 the nationalist flag waved over both Nanking and Shanghai.

The easy triumphs of their armies brought to the surface dissension within the ranks of the nationalists themselves.[9] During the occupation of central China the communists were unceasing in their agitation, and it appeared to the moderates that they were about to discard the old Kuomintang and to introduce the communist régime in its entirety. It soon appeared, however, that the left wing had badly overplayed its hand, alienating not only the moderates within the party but also large numbers of patriotic Chinese who were repelled by the economic program and by the excesses of the radicals. Chiang K'ai-shek had never betrayed communist leanings, and around himself he had assembled a group of younger nationalists who, in gen-

[9] More specifically, it was the passage-at-arms with foreigners at Nanking. When the troops were entering Nanking, in the confusion of looting and general disorder, barbarous assaults were made by nationalist soldiers upon foreigners and their property. This seems to have been a communist attempt to discredit Chiang K'ai-shek.

eral, represented the Kuomintang tradition before it had been affected by Russian influence. These established their own government at Nanking, while that of the left continued to maintain itself at Hankow. From this time on, however, the power of the communists steadily declined, in the Hankow faction as well as in the Nanking.

THE TRIUMPH OF THE NATIONALISTS

The autumn of 1927 found the nationalist movement at ebb tide. There was chaos in both wings of the party, with communists carrying on their embarrassing agitation and semi-communists industriously boring from within. To make the prospect still more discouraging, various warlords controlling one or two provinces each negotiated with different factions of the Kuomintang as his interests dictated. Disillusionment was widespread among those who had looked on the nationalist party as the salvation of China and who now beheld it the prey of factionalism and dissension.

The low estate to which the Kuomintang had fallen, however, served at least one good purpose, for weakness paved the way to reconciliation. In November a compromise between the various groups was brought about. A conference of the party reappointed Chiang K'ai-shek commander-in-chief and chairman of the central executive committee, sought to dissociate the nationalists from communism, and again enunciated the historic three principles of Sun Yat-sen as the objectives of the Kuomintang. With party unity effected, the northward march was resumed with all possible vigor. By May, 1928, the nationalist armies were drawing their net around Peking itself, and on June 1, the warlord of Manchuria and self-styled dictator of North China formally transferred the old capital to Chiang K'ai-shek.

The Kuomintang, whose program five years before had excited little more than derision, had thus become the *de facto* government of China. By January 1, 1929, not only had all of China proper accepted, at least nominally, the Nanking régime, but on December 29 the flag of the Kuomintang was officially hoisted in Manchuria as well, leaving only Mongolia and Tibet outside the nationalist federation. This does not mean, however, that the new government has established effective control over all of the territory that it professes to hold. Indeed, the route by which the Kuomintang ascended to power involved compromises of principle which have since proved costly. The triumph of the nationalists was achieved through alliances with the communists and with semi-independent military lords, —liaisons which were much easier to effect than to terminate. Moderate members of the government find themselves between the fires of the extreme radicals, whose propaganda is still being assiduously carried on, and the captains of *condottieri*, who are now demanding their reward.

Nevertheless, for the first time in more than a decade China made boast of a genuine national government. The administration which the Chinese have established at Nanking, the new capital, is admittedly undemocratic. In fact, it has a great deal in common with the Soviet government of Russia and the Fascist régime in Italy. Leaders of the Kuomintang assert, probably with justice, that to open the franchise to all would lead to disaster. During the period of "political tutelage" it is imperative that voice in the government be restricted to those best qualified to participate. In other words, the present government of China is the Kuomintang, much as that of Russia is the communist party. The central executive committee of the Kuomintang stands at the apex of the governmental pyramid. Below it is a state council, together with a group of departmental councils. In general, all of these bodies are selected from the ranks of the central executive committee. The new government of China must thus be regarded as a revolutionary oligarchy.

Whether the triumph of the Kuomintang marks the inauguration of a new era in Chinese history or whether it is merely another incident in the country's slow evolution toward stable government remains to be seen. Certainly there is nothing about the present situation to beget an easy optimism. The new régime is hemmed about by appalling problems both internal and foreign. It must establish its actual sovereignty over the nation and must demobilize the huge bodies of men who have been placed under arms during the past fifteen years. It must construct an adequate financial foundation for its rule and must suppress local chieftains who have been diverting taxes to their own use. In addition to such conspicuous tasks as these, there are a host of intangible problems, social, economic, and cultural, with which the nationalist government must deal if it is to shepherd the millions of China into twentieth century life. Yet notwithstanding the formidable obstacles in its path, the Kuomintang at least represents a government with a program and with ideals, deeply rooted in the aspirations of the Chinese people.

THE NANKING REGIME AND THE POWERS

The planks in the Kuomintang platform which appealed most strongly to the Chinese were, first, national unity, which has been nominally achieved; and secondly, the abrogation of foreign privileges in China. To the realization of the latter objective the Nanking government has proceeded with almost incontinent haste, fully conscious that no other single accomplishment would so effectively consolidate its power in the country. For on one issue and only one has China been united. Conservative and radical, the old and the new China have been unanimous in the demand that the "unequal treaties," by which foreigners have been guaranteed a privileged status, must be revised. In December, 1928, President Chiang again put his government unequivocally on record when, before a crowd of disgruntled radicals, he declared with picturesque vigor, "If within the next three years the Unequal Treaties have not been abrogated, and if by that time every foreign soldier has not left the soil of China— then, comrades, I will bow my head in shame, and you shall hew it off!"

Many provisions of the treaties with Western powers have antagonized nationalistic Chinese. Such are the arrangements for leased territories, spheres of influence, and the most-favored-nation clauses. The latter have been wholly unilateral in their application, that is, they have been applied only to the treatment which

Western powers demand of China, not to that which China may claim in the West.

Perhaps the most flagrant violations of Chinese sovereignty in the "unequal treaties" appear in two sets of provisions. In the first place, there is the extra-territorial system, the origin of which has already been sketched. Since its inception after the first Anglo-Chinese war, extra-territoriality has gradually assumed the proportions of a national disgrace, and it was scarcely to be supposed that the awakened national consciousness of China would passively accept the continuance of these privileges. In the second place, the treaties which were imposed upon China denied her one of the most elementary prerogatives of sovereignty, the right to determine her own tariff. In general, the tariff established by commercial treaties were based upon the ridiculous rate of five per cent *ad valorem*. As a result of these customs restrictions, the Chinese government has been deprived of legitimate revenue, an essential for internal reorganization, and at the same time has been prevented from raising the duties without the consent of the treaty powers. During the early part of the present century unavailing attempts to rectify this situation were made by the Chinese. The Washington conference, in spite of its conciliatory attitude toward Chinese aspirations, took no definite step in the direction of tariff autonomy.

Even before the advent of the nationalist régime, the ephemeral governments at Peking had taken measures to abrogate the odious treaties. Immediately after the war, Germany, Austria, and Russia were obliged to relinquish their extra-territorial rights. When once the Nanking government had risen to power, the movement toward treaty revision was vastly accelerated. In July, 1928, the foreign minister announced that all treaties which had expired would be abrogated and new agreements concluded, and that steps would be taken to "terminate . . . those unequal treaties which have not yet expired. . . ." This procedure, however high-handed, was extraordinarily effective. The first agreement granting tariff autonomy was signed by the United States in July, an act that was later officially stated to have constituted *de jure* recognition of the nationalist government. This accord opened the way for similar treaties with other powers, the most significant of which was Great Britain. President Chiang in his New Year's message (1929) pointed with pride to the achievements of his régime: "We have concluded treaties with twelve countries, five of whom have agreed to relinquish unequal privileges, and all are agreed on tariff autonomy." On February 1, with the consent of all of the treaty powers, the new national tariff law went into effect. The Kuomintang thus redeemed one of its pledges to the nation.

JAPAN AND THE NATIONALIST GOVERNMENT

Japan was the last power to agree to Chinese tariff autonomy, and her consent was given only at the eleventh hour. It must not be inferred, however, that the policy of Japan is one of bullying obstructionism. Since 1922 the Tokyo government apparently has been animated by a desire to deal justly with China. After the Washington conference, convinced of China's implacable hostility, deserted by Great Britain, and suspected by the United States, the Japanese discovered that a self-interest which alienated the rest of the world was not sufficiently enlightened. The present policy of Japan, therefore, is radically different from that which was exemplified by the twenty-one demands.

Nevertheless, Japan is not likely to relinquish her holdings on the continent unless her interests are protected. The Japanese are thoroughly convinced that at least an economic grip on the mainland is fundamental to their national existence. The crux of the matter is the economic crisis in which they find themselves, one that might doom any body of statesmen to sleepless nights. Essentially the problem is one of supporting a rapidly growing population on a group of islands where the amount of arable land is limited and the mineral resources meagre. Between 1867 and 1920 the population of Japan more than doubled. Obviously, if the birth-rate continues to increase, only two courses remain open to the Japanese. The first is emigration. This avenue of escape, however, has been partially closed to them by the immigration restrictions of the United States and the British possessions in the Pacific. The other possibility is to convert Japan into the factory of the East, much as Great Britain served Europe during the nineteenth century. Unfortunately, mineral resources, which the British industrialists enjoyed, are lacking to the Japanese. Consequently, they must seek their raw materials, coal, iron and oil, abroad, presumably on the continent of Asia. Furthermore, they must find their principal market in the same area. In short, Japan is driven to Chinese territory by her inexorable economic requirements. She may have abandoned her wartime policy of political imperialism, but her economic interests on the mainland are no less important to her to-day than they were a decade ago.

For these reasons, it seems doubtful whether the governments of China and Japan will be able to solve the question of Manchuria in a fashion satisfactory to both. The tenacity with which the Japanese maintain their position in that province is to be explained by political as well as by economic considerations. Tokyo well knows that beyond Manchuria there stands Russia, and that Soviet Russia, no less than Tsarist Russia, is seeking its warm-water port. At the same time, the Japanese see in Manchuria a partial solution for their economic problem. The province, which has attained a high degree of prosperity under Japanese tutelage, has absorbed many thousands of Japanese immigrants. Its fertile land and its rich mineral deposits would supply the sinews of Japanese industry and provide food for the industrial population. In any treaty that she may formulate with the Nanking government, Japan will certainly attempt to conserve her economic hold in Manchuria.

THE REVOLUTION IN CHINESE LIFE

The spectacular nature of China's political upheaval has tended to overshadow the less dramatic but perhaps more fundamental revolution taking place throughout Chinese society. Old landmarks are suffering rapid erosion and new ones are being created. Despite the quarrels of banditti and the shifting pseudo-governments, the basic patterns of Chinese life have been undergoing alteration. In some of its aspects, this economic, social, and intellectual revolution has doubtless been retarded by political conditions, but in others, the process has been accelerated by the very fact that the entire social and political order is in a state of flux.

Even the casual traveler may observe the changes which have overtaken the traditional economic life of China. The old cottage system of manufacturing is retreating before the onslaught of industrialism. Factories are being established, financed by both Chinese and foreign capital. In 1925, for example, there were in the country thirty-four iron and steel foundries, more than three million cotton spindles, and two hundred and seventy-four light and power works. Modern banks are being formed and are playing an important part in the development of the nation. The further progress of industrialism in China is partially dependent upon improved means of communication, and for the last decade railroad building has been at a standstill except in Manchuria.

The introduction of modern industry into China has been accompanied by ruthless exploitation of labor, against which the workers have sought to defend themselves, as in the West, by organization. Ephemeral labor organizations were not unknown in the earlier history of China, but contemporary conditions have lent impetus to the development of unions modeled on those of Europe and America. Prices have been rising with a rapidity out of all proportion to increases in wages, while political anarchy has prevented the enforcement of what little protective legislation has been written into the statute books. The result is that the workers have had to look to their own organizations for defense, and the recent history of China has been punctuated by periods of intense industrial strife. The new labor movement has shown its ability to act for both economic and political ends. Indeed, with their tradition of social solidarity, it is more than likely that the Chinese will surprise Westerners by their capacity for making devastating use of economic weapons such as the strike and boycott.

THE INTELLECTUAL REVOLT

Another striking consequence of the impact of the West upon China is the intellectual revolution, which has developed uninhibited since the fall of the Manchus. Until civil confusion became acute, the number of schools continued to increase, and thousands of students pursued their studies abroad. To many intellectual leaders, however, it was quite apparent that the training of the relatively few would never solve the whole problem of China, and that, in large measure, the future of the country depended upon her ability to produce an educated citizenry. It was equally evident that a high degree of literacy could never be achieved with the classical Chinese language, an enormously complicated form of expression, mastery of which was possible only to a small minority. Led by Dr. Hu Shih, an American-trained scholar, many of the Chinese intellectuals determined to use only the spoken language, a much simpler form, in their writings. Another promising attempt at language reform is that sponsored by Y. C. James Yen, who has selected from the twenty-five or thirty thousand characters in the Chinese language the one thousand most commonly used. These are being taught to the common people by ingenious methods, so that an astonishing number are attaining at least semi-literacy.

Despite their rapid absorption of much of what the West has to offer, the Chinese are no longer willing to appropriate everything upon which the Occident has placed the stamp of orthodox approval, but they are attempting to evaluate critically all institutions, both foreign and indigenous. They no longer bow in abject worship before the civilization reared in Europe and America, nor do they passively accept the superior attitudes frequently assumed by the Westerner in the Orient. The extreme current of this critical spirit is to be found in the "New Tide" or renaissance movement, which has centered in the faculty and students of the national university at Peking. In their scrutiny of Chinese institutions, even Confucianism and the family are subject to skeptical appraisal. An extraordinary degree of interest has been manifested in the liberal and radical thought of the West, Karl Marx, Kropotkin, and Tolstoy enjoying enormous popularity. The lectures of John Dewey and Bertrand Russell, both of whom spent some months in China, were enthusiastically received by the student classes. The ferment of new ideas among the students, many of whom are exceedingly callow, revealed itself in vociferous revolt against religion, capitalism, traditional morality, foreign domination, scholastic discipline, and, in short, against whatever seemed to represent the old order.

Under the stress of the economic and intellectual revolutions the Chinese social system is suffering collapse. At the foundation of the old society lay the patriarchal family, whose cohesion and effectiveness as a means of social control lay in the close association of its members. The introduction of the factory and the railroad, with the greater mobility of population which they permit, are proving incompatible with the family system. With one son working in a Hankow steel mill, for example, another in Peking, and a third in Shanghai, little restraint can be exerted by the head of the family, who may live in Foochow. Education of women has tended to produce a revolt against the older marriage customs, so that to-day marriage arrangements are increasingly settled by the young people themselves rather than by their parents. The young women, especially of the cities, are affecting the dress and manners of Western girls, the less engaging qualities along with the attractive. To put it briefly, the civilization of China, evolved out of centuries of experience and consecrated by the great Confucius himself, is being speedily and portentously altered.

This is not to say that the Chinese are about to absorb Western civilization wholesale. At one time, it seemed highly probable that the older culture might eventually disappear, but during the last decade the enthusiasm of intelligent Chinese for Occidental civilization has been tempered by a healthy skepticism. Clearly, some features of Western life must be transplanted to Chinese soil if China is to obtain her rightful place in the world. The best informed Chinese, for example, regard as inevitable and, on the whole, desirable the partial industrialization of their country, for only in this way can the material well-being of the people be made to approach Western standards. But it is becoming less and less probable that the future civilization of China will be merely a replica of that of Europe and America. If the Chinese can integrate the best of their own cultural past with the more desirable aspects of Western life, the resulting synthesis will be almost unique in the annals of civilization and will witness anew to the genius of a remarkable people.

BIBLIOGRAPHICAL NOTE

CHINA

1. CIVILIZATION

S. Wells Williams, *The Middle Kingdom*, 2 vols., New York, 1899.
The standard work on Chinese civilization.

H. B. Morse, *The Trade and Administration of China*, London, 1920.

F. H. King, *Farmers of Forty Centuries*, Madison, 1911.
Contains an excellent account of Chinese agricultural methods.

E. T. Williams, *China, Yesterday and To-day*, 4th ed., New York, 1929.

S. W. Bushell, *Chinese Art*, London, 1910.
A standard work.

T. F. Carter, *The Invention of Printing in China and Its Spread Westward*, New York, 1925.

W. S. A. Pott, *Chinese Political Philosophy*, New York, 1925.

D. T. Suzuki, *A Brief History of Early Chinese Philosophy*, London, 1914.

2. HISTORY

H. Maspero, *La Chine Antique*, Paris, 1927.

E. H. Parker, *China, Her History, Commerce, and Diplomacy*, 2nd ed., New York, 1917.

Li Ung Bing, *Outlines of Chinese History*, Shanghai, 1914.
This work has its faults, but it represents an interesting attempt on the part of a Chinese to write the history of his own country for English-speaking readers.

Latourette, K. S., *The Development of China*, 4th ed., Boston, 1929.
A brief, readable account of Chinese history. Contains admirable interpretive passages.

JAPAN

1. CIVILIZATION

F. Brinkley, *Japan, Its History, Arts, and Literature*, 8 vols. The standard work.

B. H. Chamberlain, *Things Japanese*, 4th ed., London, 1902. A guide to Japanese civilization. Topics arranged alphabetically.

Lafcadio Hearn, *Japan, An Attempt at Interpretation*, New York, 1904.
A beautifully written, somewhat sentimentalized description of Japanese civilization.

Inazo Nitobé, *Bushido, The Soul of Japan*, 10th ed., New York, 1906.
A readable, but somewhat idealized picture of Japanese chivalry.

Etsu Sugimoto, *A Daughter of the Samurai*, New York, 1925.
A delightful autobiography of life in Japan during the period of transition.

2. HISTORY

James Murdoch, *A History of Japan*, 3 vols., Tokyo, Kobe, New York, 1903-26.
When completed, this work will probably be the standard history of Japan.

W. W. McLaren, *A Political History of Japan During the Meiji Era*, 1867-1912, New York, 1916.

K. S. Latourette, *The Development of Japan*, New York, 1918.
Brief, accurate, and readable.

K. Hara, *An Introduction to the History of Japan*, New York, 1920.
One of the best of the brief histories

RELATIONS BETWEEN THE EAST AND THE WEST

Tyler Dennett, *Americans in Eastern Asia*, New York, 1922.
  The standard account of American policy in the Orient.

H. B. Morse, *International Relations of the Chinese Empire*, 1834-1911, 3 vols., London, 1910-18.
  A monumental study compiled chiefly from British sources.

H. B. Morse and H. F. MacNair, *Far Eastern International Relations*, Shanghai, 1928.
  An abridgment of the preceding work, with additional discussion of events in the Far East to 1928.

A. J. Sargent, *Anglo-Chinese Commerce and Diplomacy*, London, 1907.
  An admirable analysis.

A. Reichwein, *China and Europe*, New York, 1925.
  "Intellectual and artistic contacts in the eighteenth century" is the subtitle.

P. J. Treat, *The Far East*, New York, 1928.
  Concerned chiefly with China and Japan after their contact with the West. Deals only with political and diplomatic aspects.

H. M. Vinacke, *A History of the Far East in Modern Times*, New York, 1928.
  Includes especially useful chapters on cultural changes in the East.

K. S. Latourette, *A History of Christian Missions in China*, New York, 1929.
  An authoritative study.

RECENT EVENTS AND TENDENCIES IN THE FAR EAST

R. L. Buell, *The Washington Conference*, New York, 1922.
  The best general account.

Yamato Ichihashi, *The Washington Conference and After*, Stanford University, 1928.
  A sympathetic treatment of Japanese policy.

H. T. Hodgkin, *China in the Family of Nations*, New York, 1923.

Lays special emphasis on industrial and intellectual changes.

S. K. Hornbeck, *Contemporary Politics in the Far East*, New York, 1916.

An excellent study.

H. K. Norton, *China and the Powers*, New York, 1928.

One of the best of the many recent books on international politics in the Far East.

F. W. Price, Trans., *San Min Chu I*, Shanghai, 1927.

A translation of Sun Yat-sen's volume on the "Three Principles" of the Kuomintang.

T'ang Leang-li, *The Foundations of Modern China*, London, 1928.

A statement of the Kuomintang point of view.

T. T. Lew and others, *China To-day, Through Chinese Eyes*, 2nd ed., London, 1927.

INDEX